The Paired Maths Handbook

Parental Involvement and Peer Tutoring in Mathematics

Keith Topping and Judi Bamford

David Fulton Publishers

London

David Fulton Publishers Ltd
Ormond House, 26–27 Boswell Street, London WC1N 3JD

First published in Great Britain by David Fulton Publishers 1998

British Library Cataloguing in Publication Data
A catalogue record for this book is available from the British Library

ISBN 1–85346–497–X

Typeset by FSH, London
Printed in Great Britain by Bell and Bain Ltd, Glasgow

Contents

Preface

This book is one of a family of three related books, consisting of two resource Handbooks for everyday use, supported by a more detailed background text for deeper reading and reference.

The three Paired Maths and Science books

The Paired Maths Handbook (by Keith Topping and Judi Bamford) gives a brief introduction to the rationale, materials, organisation and evaluation of the Paired Maths method for parental involvement and peer tutoring in mathematics, for children aged 4 to 14. This is followed by 12 different practical resources to copy to help with the organisation of the method. The main part of the book consists of two-dimensional mathematical games to copy, complete with instructions and needing minimal other materials. These games are particularly suitable for children aged 9 to 12, especially when involved in cooperative learning or peer tutoring in schools or other study centres. This is the book you are reading now.

The Paired Science Handbook (by Keith Topping) gives a brief introduction to the rationale, history, materials, organisation and evaluation of the Paired Science method for parental involvement and peer tutoring in science. This is followed by eight different resources to copy to help with organisation. The main part consists of Paired Science Activity Sheets to copy, complete with instructions for children and helpers, and needing little equipment other than that already available in most homes and schools. These Activity Sheets are particularly suitable for children aged 5 to 7, especially when engaged in parental involvement projects linking home and school, (although they can also be used in cross-age peer tutoring in schools or other study centres up to the age of 11, and with older children with difficulties with science).

The more detailed background text (by Keith Topping and Judi Bamford) is titled *Parental Involvement and Peer Tutoring in Mathematics and Science*. Its subtitle *Developing Paired Maths into Paired Science* indicates that its main focus is the Paired Maths method, which has a longer history and wider research than the more recent Paired Science work. However, much of the rationale and many of the organisational issues and possible applications are common to both, and the implications for Paired Science are also explored throughout the book. Co-ordinators of parent involvement or peer tutoring projects and maths and science specialists or coordinators will find the practical guidance in this book about materials, organisation and evaluation essential reading. More information is also included about related international developments and research findings, and extension of the methods to more challenging target groups.

More about this book

The book you are now reading is of course the first of the family described above – The Paired Maths Handbook. This practical handbook for teachers and parents shows how to consolidate and deepen mathematical understanding and ability, and improve motivation and confidence, in children aged 4 to 14, by involving parents or older children at home and peers in schools as tutors.

Practical experience of mathematical exploration, collaboration and competition with supportive discussion and feedback helps children generalise their problem-solving skills to 'real-life' everyday community settings. Enjoyment, motivation and confidence is heightened in *all* participant partners, while still maintaining linkage to National Curriculum attainment targets.

Paired Maths is equally suitable for 'ordinary' children or those with special needs, whether as tutees or tutors. The method is based on years of field work in England and Scotland. Paired Maths and Paired Science both have their roots in Paired Reading, which also gave rise to Cued Spelling and Paired Writing (Topping 1995).

Structure of the book

Section A gives a brief introduction to the methods of Paired Maths, outlining the rationale and development, describing selecting and creating materials at the three different levels, offering guidance for organising successful parental involvement and peer tutoring projects, touching on the evaluation evidence and considering how to evaluate Paired Maths projects. All of these issues are discussed in much greater depth in the supporting text: *Parental Involvement and Peer Tutoring in Mathematics and Science* (Topping and Bamford 1998). However, there should be enough information in this Handbook to enable the reader to see how to use the reproducible organisational resources in Section B and/or the games in Section C, and make a start.

In Section B, the reproducible resources for setting up Paired Maths start with an Organisational Checklist to complete – it is especially important not to forget anything when organising a parental involvement project. This is followed by a brief 'What to do' Parent Leaflet and a more extended 'Further Hints' Parent Leaflet. Diary and Language Cards for keeping track of game use and the language involved are provided, together with a Games Loan Record Chart and a poster of core mathematical vocabulary suitable for home or school. A set of questionnaires to help with evaluation include examples for parents and for teachers. There is also an Extended Joint Evaluation Questionnaire for children, parents and peers and a 'feelings' questionnaire for Paired Maths in class with peers. Finally, examples of linkages to English National Curriculum mathematics attainment targets are provided for Key Stage 1 and Key Stage 3.

Section C incorporates a substantial number of two-dimensional maths games, including many reproducible maths game boards. Reproducible instructions and notes of other materials needed (e.g. playing pieces, counters) are provided on separate pages for maximum flexibility. Do not stick the instructions on the back of the boards! These games are Level 3 games, particularly suitable for children aged 9 to 12, especially when involved in cooperative learning or peer tutoring in schools or other study centres (although they can also be used in parental involvement, and with older children with difficulties with maths). The games include ancient games from many countries of the world as well as more recent ones, all in the public domain. Games are categorised into five areas: 1. Strategy, 2. Space, 3. Number, 4. Puzzles, and 5. Extension Games of a particularly fiendish nature.

Additional instructions are provided for games which merely require the addition of an ordinary pack of playing cards.

Audience for the book

This book is directed at teachers and those who train, support and manage teachers. It is also directed at parents, who can do Paired Maths at home without any support from school if necessary, although working in partnership is preferable.

Acknowledgements

Very many colleagues contributed to the work described in this book and its companion volumes, but we particularly acknowledge the invaluable input of Tiny Arora (currently Associate Tutor to the postgraduate professional training course in educational psychology at the University of Sheffield and Senior Educational Psychologist in the Kirklees Education Support Service in West Yorkshire), Anne Mallinson (an Educational Psychologist with the Stirling Psychological Service in Scotland), and Kay Shanahan, (the In-service Training Coordinator and a class teacher at Highfields Special School in Huddersfield, West Yorkshire).

Keith Topping
Judi Bamford
January 1998

Bibliography

Topping, K. J. (1995) *Paired Reading, Spelling and Writing: The Handbook for Teachers and Parents*. London and New York: Cassell.

Topping, K. J. (1998) *The Paired Science Handbook: Parental Involvement and Peer Tutoring in Science*. London: David Fulton Publishers; Bristol PA: Taylor & Francis.

Topping, K. J. and Bamford, J. (1998) *The Paired Maths Handbook: Parental Involvement and Peer Tutoring in Mathematics*. London: David Fulton Publishers; Bristol PA: Taylor & Francis.

Topping, K. J. and Bamford, J. (1998) *Parental Involvement and Peer Tutoring in Mathematics and Science: Developing Paired Maths into Paired Science*. London: David Fulton Publishers; Bristol PA: Taylor & Francis.

Section A:
Introduction to Paired Maths

Introduction to Paired Maths

What is Paired Maths? What do you need to implement it? How do you organise it? How do you know it works? All these questions are answered in this section – but first another question: why?

Rationale and development

The importance of maths

Maths is (or should be) useful and important throughout life. Numeracy matters. Poor numeracy skills are a major disadvantage in everyday life and in the job market. However, it cannot be assumed that more of the same sort of teaching in school would solve the problem, since there is also concern about the relationship between the school mathematics curriculum and the mathematical demands of everyday life and employment. For the research supporting these assertions (and others following), refer to the more detailed supporting text *Parental Involvement and Peer Tutoring in Mathematics and Science* (Topping and Bamford 1998).

National Standards

Over the years considerable concern has been expressed about the performance of British and US children in mathematics at both primary (elementary) and secondary (high) level, when compared to the performance of children from other countries, particularly those on the Pacific Rim. At best, our standards seem be staying the same, while other countries overtake.

Government Reports

The Cockcroft Report (1982) was an important landmark for mathematics education in the UK. It recognised and emphasised the importance of parental influence and the early age by which attitudes to mathematics are fixed: 'by the end of the primary years a child's attitude to mathematics is often becoming fixed . . . and for many this meant being fixed as an attitude of rejection and antagonism'. It defined the aims of mathematics teaching as developing powers of logical thought as well as equipping children with numerical skills.

Attitudes to maths and gender stereotypes

Even in middle class areas, many parents see themselves as bad at mathematics and hated it at school, especially at secondary level. Thus disliking mathematics can all too readily be construed as 'normal'. Gender stereotypes can also be transmitted within the home (as well as at school), possibly leading girls to abandon interest in mathematics even though they are no less capable. Consequently, 'parental involvement in maths' schemes which merely 'ship home the curriculum' have been criticised as naïvely ignoring the affective and historical dimensions of parents' own reality. There is a danger of parents' modelling negative attitudes to mathematics which are then adopted by children and become a self-fulfilling prophecy. Paired Maths is designed to help deal with this.

How mathematics is learned

Skemp (1971, 1978, 1989) suggested that because many mathematics learners lacked self-confidence and were insecure in their understanding, they relied on habit-learning, rather than developing generalisable concepts or models. Children were too concerned with giving the right answers to a limited class of questions – 'tricks for ticks' – with very little encouragement to relate these recipes to their concrete experience.

For Skemp, the essence of intelligent learning was adaptability – being able to learn from encounters with the physical world, matching experience against expectation, communicating with and learning from others and comparing ideas with them, and being able to develop and build mathematical models which yielded creative and testable predictions. Many of these precepts are now embodied in the English National Curriculum, but not necessarily operationalised in classroom practice. The approach recommended by Skemp was activity- and game-based, with an emphasis on discussion and cooperation. Paired Maths is exactly this.

The definition of mathematics

Similarly, Nunes and Bryant (1996) emphasised that mathematics is a contextually and socially defined activity. 'School' mathematics can all too easily consist only of applications and purposes, methodologies and solutions which are socially approved within the context of the classroom by the dominant cultural influence – the teacher. The result of the discontinuity between the classroom and 'real life' can be that the child's conception of what mathematics *is* narrows – and the child can be disempowered.

Language in mathematics

In attempting to start from the child's own point of departure in terms of understanding, the role of discussion is widely seen as crucial. Paired Maths activities with peers enable a lower threshold of self-disclosure and give the teacher the opportunity to circulate to diagnose misconception by strategic overhearing. Something similar might be true for some parents at home.

As with other curricular areas (e.g. science), information transfer and processing is heavily dependent upon language. Mathematics has much specialist vocabulary, including that applied to abstract and complex concepts, as well as using some 'everyday' vocabulary with more specific and restricted meanings. Concept formation is aided greatly by the ability to accurately use the related language, while the learning of new concepts is closely associated with the acquisition of new words which are meaningful. However, children might learn words without really understanding the associated concepts, while their understanding of some concepts might be underestimated because they do not use the 'official' terminology. In Paired Maths the games readily stimulate discussion of joint and purposeful concrete activities, requiring children to use and understand words and phrases in a mathematical context.

Maths games

Games have other advantages. Strong support or scaffolding of the parent-child or peer tutor-tutee interaction is needed in maths activities. The structured rules and materials of games provide this, while avoiding any danger of a didactic 'top–down' ethos. This is much less threatening than being told what is wrong by the teacher, and much less likely to lead to the 'tricks for ticks' mentality. Games also promote active involvement, are intrinsically motivating, exciting and challenging, are grounded in concrete meaningful experience and have a purpose in which the child is intimately engaged, promoting greater concentration and persistence as well as decision-making and problem-solving.

Paired Maths games require children to think and do more mentally than they could possibly record on paper in the same time. They enable repetition for consolidation while avoiding tedium. Success or failure is self-evident, so they are self-correcting – no 'marking' is required. Games can be played at different levels and the element of chance enables children of all abilities to be included and all children to have an equal likelihood of success. The inherent enjoyment and success can foster positive attitudes to the self and to mathematics. They also encourage turn-taking, cooperation, communication, and other interpersonal skills.

Other factors in effectiveness

The value of peer assisted learning is emphasised by Topping and Ehly (1998), who list other possible factors which might account for the success of Paired Maths.

Intellectually, these could include increases (for helpers, helped, or both) in:

- attention,
- time on task and engagement,
- positive practice,
- fluency,
- modelling,
- prompting,
- immediacy and timeliness of tutor intervention,

- individualisation of learning,
- individual accountability and responsibility,
- planning and rehearsal,
- reorganisation of thinking,
- explaining with examples in vernacular language,
- questioning intelligently and adaptively,
- predicting and estimating,
- prevention of overload in information processing,
- responding opportunities,
- identification of gaps and filling them,
- error disclosure and analysis,
- self-correction,
- feedback,
- reinforcement, and
- self-assessment and self-regulation.

Attitudinally, these might include:

- variety and interest,
- activity and inter-activity,
- modelling of enthusiasm and coping,
- identification and bonding,
- ownership of the learning process, and
- self-confidence, self-belief and self-efficacy.

Related programmes

Various types of programmes to involve parents and other carers in the mathematical development of their children have become more common throughout the world (further details in Topping and Bamford 1998). The 'Family Math' programme has proved very popular in the USA and Canada and has extended to parts of Australia. In the UK, Graham's 'Sums for Mums' project was followed by Parent Resource in Support of Maths (PRISM). The IMPACT project, widely known in the UK, involves the class teacher sending home mathematical activities which parent and child carry out together (Merttens and Vass 1987, 1993). It is closely tied to traditional classroom activities which the child exports to the home, often involving whole classes completing the same 'homework' simultaneously. This enables the activity to be closely articulated to current class teaching, but is a more 'top–down' approach. Surprisingly, given its high profile, little evaluation evidence on IMPACT other than the anecdotal appears to be publicly available. There is also a considerable related background literature on cooperative learning in maths and peer tutoring in maths, (again, more details in Topping and Bamford 1998).

The history and development of Paired Maths

A surge in enthusiasm for parental involvement in reading at the beginning of the 1980s led to a variety of methods for parental involvement and peer tutoring in literacy (Topping and Wolfendale 1985, Wolfendale and Topping 1996). In the Kirklees Psychological Service in the Kirklees Education Authority in West Yorkshire, specific structured methods such as Paired Reading, Cued Spelling and Paired Writing were designed or extended and evaluated (see Topping 1995). These methods proved very effective, durable and easy for schools to use, and spread to a majority of schools in the authority as well as nationally and internationally.

The Multiply Attainments Through Home Support (MATHS) project was launched in Kirklees – the beginnings of Paired Maths as reported in this book. Many schools had already been successful with Paired Reading, and from this foundation were confident to proceed with Paired Maths. As with other Paired methods, the delivery of a first Paired Maths project in collaboration with a school was also intended as a form of participatory in-service training for the teachers.

The activities and format were designed to be non-threatening to either teachers or parents, both in content and teaching implications. The projects aimed to reinforce for teachers, through explication to parents, the importance of language and non-computational activities in understanding and practising mathematical concepts. This form of in-service training was thus both direct and indirect, applied to the teachers through the parents.

Unlike the Paired approaches in literacy, Paired Maths used specified materials (games), necessitated by the width and complexity of the area and the very limited confidence of many parents (and teachers) in it. Kits of mathematical games were assembled for this purpose, which were loaned to schools as part of 'pump-priming', after which schools were expected to create their own in-house kit for subsequent projects.

Much of the early Paired Maths work involved parental tutoring using kits of mathematical games appropriate to children aged 4 to 7. Projects were generally targeted on mixed-ability classes in mainstream schools, rather than on children with difficulties, this being necessitated by principles of equal opportunity and serving to avoid any stigmatisation.

Later, the contents of this Key Stage 1 kit were revised, and kits different in structure and content were developed for 'Junior' age children (7 to 11, Key Stage 2), and for lower secondary age children (11 to 13, Key Stage 3), with the expectation that older children would be increasingly likely to use these in peer based projects in schools. Peer and parent projects began to be operated across this wider age range.

Many more schools showed interest in developing projects, including schools for children with learning difficulties. In multicultural schools, the language content of Paired Maths was found very valuable for families whose first language was not English. In parallel, the extension of Paired Learning into science was undertaken, described in *The Paired Science Handbook* (Topping 1998).

Why Paired Maths is different

In summary, the particularly distinctive features of the system of Paired Maths include:

- a very strong focus on developing more positive attitudes to mathematics and to the self as a mathematician, increasing enthusiasm and confidence in all participants (child or adult), rather than a preoccupation with specific official maths knowledge. Maths is about feelings, too.

- a very strong focus on the value of the existing home and community mathematical culture and competencies, with the aim of building on those competencies to enable parents and children to meet their own needs. Maths is for life.
- an emphasis on self-selection and choice for maximum individualisation and personal relevance, and through that high motivation. Maths is about me.
- a systemic approach involving reciprocal interaction and feedback with inbuilt intrinsic rewards for all players. No-one is as smart as all of us.
- a systemic approach which enables the offering of equal opportunities and access to all members of all families of all kinds. We all get to play.

Thus the Paired Maths system blends selected elements of good practice together into a package which is economical, robust and durable as well as dynamic, inclusive and effective, with a particular focus on feelings, relevance to individual life needs and mutual and lifelong learning.

Materials

Principles behind successful games

Experience showed that ideally games should meet the following criteria. They should:

- be enjoyable,
- allow equal competition or cooperation between child and parent or peer,
- be easy to understand,
- be flexible and allow extension,
- encourage discussion,
- not look like school work or encourage a didactic approach,
- be physically attractive,
- be robust physically,
- be well-packaged and easily kept together and complete,
- be safe, and
- be inexpensive.

The games should place demands on mathematical skills, but outcomes should also be subject to an element of random chance or luck. Three-dimensional games are generally much less like schoolwork and much more like 'Christmas presents', and therefore more motivating for all children, as well as more developmentally appropriate for young children.

If games involve as many as possible of the senses (through activities such as speaking, listening, watching, touching, moving and even smelling and tasting), they are likely to be accessible to more children of different abilities and cultural and linguistic backgrounds. However, they should not incorporate irrelevant distraction. They should not be too big, or they will prove difficult to store and transport home. The game itself should reasonably brief – especially for peer projects. Games need clear rules for play which are not too long, nor too difficult to read or follow –

and the game does need to have a clear sense of purpose. Obviously, the games chosen should be appropriate to the chronological age or developmental level of the children who will be playing them. However, it is even better if they can be played at various different levels of complexity.

Development of the Level 1 games kits

The first (Level 1) Paired Maths projects were aimed at children aged 5 to 7, and eventually over 40 different games were accumulated. Included were some of the traditional games that grandparents remember playing before the days of television (e.g. Ludo, Snakes and Ladders, Dominoes, Beetle and Draughts), all providing opportunities for meaningful counting, one-to-one matching and addition. Others (such as Tangrams and Rods) would perhaps have been more familiar to teachers of young children. Each game was accompanied by a list of activities to do with the materials, a list of words to be used and a Diary/Record Sheet (see Section B4).

For children of this age, the English National Curriculum conceptualises mathematics as divided into major fields:

- number;
- shape, space and measures;
- using and applying mathematics; and
- handling data.

The Paired Maths Level 1 games were grouped into six more differentiated categories: Matching, Conservation, Counting, Shape, Pattern, and Ordering.

These six categories related neatly to a six-week project in which participants were asked to chose one game from a different category each week. For ease of differentiation, each category was colour-coded, so participants knew a red-coded game had to be returned to the red-coded box, and that they could not then take another red game. This ensured that they sampled a wide range of mathematical activities and avoided reinforcing a narrow conceptualisation of what maths entails and embraces. It also enabled the mathematical language in play with each game to be focused on a limited set of highly relevant key words. This was more manageable for the parents, and over the whole project children would be cumulatively exposed to the complete range of language (see Section B6). Games were categorised by their most prominent conceptual content. However, many games actually covered more than one conceptual area of mathematics, so categorisation could be somewhat arbitrary. The final, full listing was:

Counting	Matching	Shape
Snakes and Ladders	Three to Match	Pass the Bag
Ludo	Huff Puff	Shapes
Insey Winsey Spider	Humpty Dumpty	Tessellation
Scaredy Cat	Memo	Mr Space Game
Beggar my Neighbour	Dominoes	Tangrams
Blackpool card game	Beetle	Jigsaw
Leapfrog	Snap (various forms)	Attribute Bingo
Cat and Mouse	Bingo	Dotty Triangles

Pattern	Conservation	Ordering
Ladybirds	Rods	Rummy
Pick a Button	Button Box	Halves & Quarters
Mosaics	Connect 4 (Rows)	The Old Woman who
Happy Families	Dogimoes	Lived in a Shoe
3 Men's Morris	Choose a Pattern	Hundred Square Jigsaw
Nine Holes	Three at a Time	Crossing Game
		Beanstalk/Dragon

Section B11 outlines the National Curriculum linkages in further detail for this level. More details of these three-dimensional games will be found in Topping and Bamford (1998) – especially Appendix 1a.

Development of the Level 2 games kits

The categories for the next level, Key Stage 2 (children aged 7 to 11), were somewhat different: Bonds, Relations, Shape, Strategy, and Puzzles (cross-area). This reflected developmental patterns of mathematical growth in children, and the related difference in Key Stage 2 terminology in the National Curriculum. The early emphasis on Conservation, Matching and Counting was seen as leading to work on Number Bonds and Relationships. The early emphasis on Ordering and Pattern led toward Strategy. The Shape category remained, at a higher level of operation. Puzzles were included as examples of cross-area activities, which could be enjoyed by just one child if preferred or necessitated. A choice was left from any area for the sixth week. A full listing of titles of games included will be found in Appendix 1b in Topping and Bamford (1998).

Development of the Level 3 games kits

At the next level, the games kits were more likely to be used in peer projects in class than for parental involvement. To ensure sufficient variety, the kits were enlarged by the inclusion of many two-dimensional ancient or modern public domain games, playable with a board and/or other simple equipment. Reproducible examples of these will be found in Section C, and a full listing in Appendix 1c of Topping and Bamford (1998). However, it must be emphasised that the Level 3 kits also contained some three-dimensional games, which were still greatly appreciated by these older participant children. The categorical structure showed further change from the kits for younger children: Number, Space, Strategy, Solitaire or Cooperative Puzzles, and Extension games. The latter were more complex games intended to challenge the more able.

Most of the games were however oriented toward the lower end of Key Stage 3. 'Number' included counting, bonds, sequence, order, computation (arithmetic) and probability. Strategy games involved a large element of deduction and prediction leading to the generation of strategies, in many cases requiring an algebraic understanding of the mathematical principles involved. Space games incorporated a large element of visuo-spatial perception and organisation, an appreciation of shape, pattern and geometry, in two and three dimensions and with reference to solids, and including locations and transformation in space.

Puzzles covered all areas. Some were very hard! The increased emphasis on individual puzzles ensured that where there was a heterogeneous group in class, and perhaps erratic attendance patterns, individuals could operate alone at certain times. However, many of these 'solitaire' puzzles proved fascinating to others, and cooperative problem-solving pairs or groups often formed spontaneously even without teacher suggestion. In these games the discussion became directed along the lines of why and how the puzzle worked and how it could be improved.

All five boxes required skills in data handling and the organisation of information (although not necessarily written record keeping) and skill in the application and generalisation of mathematical principles. In relation to National Curriculum requirements, the Key Stage 3 kit was particularly strong on application and approximation, prediction and probability, strategy and spatial aspects – and especially on problem-solving at speed. The kit was relatively light on written recording, decimals, fractions, percentages, measuring and working with very large numbers. Section B12 outlines the National Curriculum linkages in greater detail for this level.

Sources of games

Games kits were initially loaned to schools for their first project. Once this was under way, schools involved parents in fund-raising, in making games, in searching car boot sales and writing to manufacturers for sample games in order to provide their own kits for future projects. Teachers also scoured the darker recesses of the school for relevant materials which were no longer being used in class.

Many of the games listed in the three kit Levels are commercially available. Some games are for four people and can be split into two, providing two sets to borrow. However, manufacturers are constantly looking for novelty. Often the games are taken off the market or replaced with alternatives, so the basic principles of selection have to be applied each time a new kit is made up. More games will be found in commercial outlets in the months before Christmas – although it is difficult for teachers to find time for games hunting during this period. Many games suppliers have a mail order facility (although with the attendant problem of not being able to inspect the goods). Addresses of games suppliers will be found in Appendix 2 of Topping and Bamford (1998), and a list of books including mathematical games in Appendix 3.

Increasingly, maths schemes commercially produced for schools include some 'games', and perhaps even take-home activities for 'parental involvement', but these should be scrutinised and evaluated carefully, as they often prove to be rather dreary, repetitive and didactic.

Organisation

Key issues involved in organising a project include:

- establishing objectives,
- selecting target groups,
- recruiting parent or peer tutors,

- organising access to games or activities,
- controlling experience of various areas of mathematics or science, and
- running a training or 'launch' meeting.

With peer projects, there is the added issue of selection and matching of partners. Further important issues of organisation include:

- monitoring the ongoing activities,
- trouble-shooting,
- feedback of evaluation results, and
- keeping the momentum going.

Remember the first project must be a resounding success – for the children, the parents, the neighbourhood grapevine and (not least) for you. Start off small and invest time to ensure success for all.

Section B1 provides an Organisational Checklist of the issues that will need to be considered for parental involvement projects, with space for decisions to be inserted as they are made. The completed checklist can then be copied to all interested and involved parties.

Consider your context: any special strengths on which to capitalise, or any special difficulties to deal with? Consult with all relevant parties. Set clear and realistic objectives: intellectual, attitudinal, social or a combination of these. Don't try to solve all the worst problems with your first effort.

Decide on target pupils – both type (ages, classes, abilities) and number to be invited to participate. Involving parents is easier with younger children. Take care to avoid any stigmatisation of the project as 'just for slow ones'.

Determine how many games of what Level you will need to have available for your expected participant group – make sure you have them in stock, categorised and labelled in time. Make very sure the instructions will be readable by the people who will need to use them. Consider where they can be accessibly stored. Keep a supply of spare dice, playing pieces, etc.

In peer projects, operation within one regular class is easiest: cross age is more difficult. Match children into pairs. Usually aim for heterogeneous maths ability in the pairing, but aim for a modest ability differential rather than a big one. All participants should find some cognitive challenge in their joint activities and the tutor should be 'learning by teaching'. Certainly ensure that one partner is a capable reader of instructions. (However, for puzzles and extension games, same-ability pairing can work well, provided complex instructions can be read.)

Consider whether to match pairs within or across gender – and what the adverse effects of either might be. If undecided, go for across gender. Avoid matching children who are already good friends, as this can lead to much off-task behaviour. Expect initial squabbles in a few pairs – only re-pair after 2 to 3 weeks if all else fails. Consider how you will deal with non-attendance – some re-pairing might be necessitated then. Re-pairing for everyone much later to introduce novelty might be considered.

Peer projects can operate in lesson time, or as part of support time or lunchtime Maths Clubs, or even in after school 'homework centres' or 'supported study centres' (see Chapter 6 in Topping and Bamford 1998; you might also find *The Peer*

Tutoring Handbook, Topping 1988, useful for background reading). A minimum core of Paired Maths in timetabled class time is always valuable, not least to ensure continuity and give the project credibility. In peer projects, pupil monitors can help distribute games and record cards, etc.

There needs to be a basic agreement between teacher, parent (tutor) and child (tutee) to play maths games for a short period of time for several sessions per week over a period of six weeks. Especially with parent projects, involve the local media, as an aid to subsequent recruitment.

Remember, pairs must initially take any activity *from a different area* each week. The experience of most schools is that a six-week project fits readily into half a term, so that there is no difficulty with the holiday breaks.

Establish a way of keeping games or activities together according to the conceptual area. Boxes with different coloured stickers for each area and a different number for each game within an area gives a helpful coding system. Provide plastic bags for carrying games between home and school.

The child's choice of game or activity needs to be recorded on a Games Loan or Activity Record Chart (see Section B5). In Level 1 Paired Maths with younger children, when the game is chosen an accompanying Diary and Language Record Card (also colour-coded) goes home with the game (see Section B4). This is then returned with the game at the end of the week, for the teacher to look at and countersign or add a comment.

Once the project starts, most participants are happy to do the checking in and out themselves. However, there will need to be someone available at 'game exchange time' to discuss choices, oversee returns, answer questions, listen to experiences and help to solve problems. When the game or activity chosen has proved impossible to live with for a week, some facility for 'emergency' early exchange is helpful.

Invitations to the 'launch' meeting can now be sent out. For parents, parallel meetings during the day and in the evening might be necessary. With parents, an informal setting is best – they will be anxious. The provision of tea or coffee at the outset helps ease the interaction. The parents (tutors) should sit around tables with a number of games or activities and try them out with each other. The target children (tutees) can be brought in later, once the parents (tutors) feel more familiar and comfortable with the situation.

Talk to the whole group about the rationale of the project, especially about enjoyment, while emphasising the underlying mathematical or scientific concepts and relating these to the participants' own experience. Mathematics is not just computation: it is learning about relationships, patterns and shapes. Point out that not many people say that they like maths, and parents can easily pass a negative or defeatist attitude on to their children. However, adults often actually competently use a wide range of different types of mathematical activity in their everyday lives. Of equal importance is the use of the games to explore and understand the specific mathematical use of language.

This is an ideal point at which to bring the children in to the meeting. The main points can then be recapitulated and summarised (as if just for the children's benefit).

A discussion of the games, with a practical demonstration of at least one, is now needed, with clarification of the mathematical concepts and language involved. The day-to-day commitment and organisational arrangements involved in joining the project can now be detailed. Partners need to be told where the games will be kept, what days and times are scheduled for game exchange, who the key people are in school to ask for help and advice, and how to record which games have been borrowed.

Outline opportunities for access to ongoing support and encouragement, especially at exchange time. Parents (and tutors) may also need advice about playing games at different levels. Advise that missing or damaged games or pieces should always be reported (some wear and tear is inevitable and no blame will attach), since otherwise the next pair will receive an unplayable game.

Towards the end of the meeting, deal with any remaining questions. At the end, a leaflet should be given to the family which reminds them of the main points (see Sections B2 and B3). These leaflets can also serve as part of the 'script' for a slightly nervous teacher conducting their first launch meeting. Do not however give out the leaflets early in the meeting, as reading will interfere with listening. Partners should leave the meeting with a game, Diary and Language Card (if Level 1), explanatory leaflet, details of exchange arrangements and the date of the follow-up meeting.

During the course of the project, the coordinating teacher will check Diary and Language Cards and discuss with participants whenever possible to check that all is going well. In a peer project, the teacher can of course easily directly observe Paired Maths taking place, and is available to stimulate discussion and ensure no false assumptions, personal friction, or other deviations develop.

The subsequent follow-up meeting enables exchange of feedback between parents (tutors), teachers and (sometimes) children, leading to evaluation of the project and consideration of onward progression, possible improvements and further planning. Try to avoid domination of the meeting by the most vocal. As soon as the parents arrive they could be asked to complete a Parent Evaluation Questionnaire (see Section B7), which will help them to focus on some of the questions to be discussed.

Many parents and children may well wish the project to continue in some form, albeit less intensively. Each family or set of partners should feel able to make whatever choice seems right for them – and of course reserve the right to change their minds. If they wish to continue after the trial period, they have complete free choice across all areas, and can pursue their own current enthusiasms.

The meeting needs to be a celebration of all the commitment and continuing involvement that has been shown. Certificates or badges for the children can be a part of this. For the parents a pocket book of ideas for further maths games could be given as a 'thank you' offering and stimulus to continue.

An initial lukewarm response is not unusual in communities where families have learnt to see the school as an institution and teachers as authority figures who blame parents rather than help them. Don't worry – once your first project has been successful (as it must be), the word will begin to spread through the community. You might end up with more interest than you can manage!

Background research evidence

There is a good deal of background research relevant to the Paired Maths approach, but space does not permit detailed discussion of it here (see Topping and Bamford 1998 for more).

Maths games

The use of maths games in class is now considered a mainstream activity, recommended in the National Curriculum in England and the 5–14 Curriculum in Scotland (indeed, games and puzzles are mentioned as 'required' resources in the latter). Research has demonstrated that some (but not all) games increase the use of mathematical language and lead to gains in mathematical ability. One of the better studies showed maths test gains which were sustained at follow-up and transferred to other areas, while another controlled study with children with learning difficulties also showed gains.

Cooperative learning

Davidson has provided several reviews of research on small group cooperative learning in mathematics (Davidson 1985, 1989; Davidson and Kroll 1991) and a handbook of readings for teachers (Davidson 1990). Forming groups heterogeneous in ability is usual. He suggested (1985) that gains from more traditional cooperative learning of mathematics were only consistently found for computational skills, simple concepts and application problems.

Peer tutoring

The effectiveness of peer tutoring in general has been widely acknowledged for many years, as various reviews and meta-analyses have indicated (Sharpley and Sharpley 1981, Cohen *et al.* 1982, Topping 1988, Topping and Ehly 1998). Britz and his colleagues (1989) reviewed the effects of peer tutoring specifically on mathematics performance. Cross-age and same-age, classwide and reciprocal peer tutoring in mathematics have all demonstrated good results. In summary, peer tutoring in mathematics has been shown to yield significant achievement gains on both criterion- and norm-referenced mathematics tests, and gains in attitudes to mathematics, self-concept and social interaction, especially with at-risk, socially disadvantaged and low achieving children. Gains for both tutors and tutees are evident. Gains are more likely to be substantial with training and experience for participants. Extending to also include parental involvement appears to have a further additive effect.

Parental involvement in maths in North America

Although a substantial number of projects have been reported, finding hard evaluative evidence is more difficult. Brodsky and his colleagues (1994) conducted a controlled evaluation of two successive years of a short series of 'Family Math' programmes. Experimental children with prior Family Math experience showed higher gains on standardised mathematics performance measures than other groups, but only two of the analyses showed statistical significance. Family Math parents did show increased general involvement with their children's schools and the parents and teachers were very positive about the programme.

Parental involvement in maths in the UK

A number of small projects in the UK have nevertheless shown encouraging results, especially as three were controlled studies. Children involved ranged from very young primary school children to high school pupils, mostly but not exclusively those with mathematics difficulties. Gains were demonstrated on various kinds of tests, although not all gains reached statistical significance – this being elusive with small samples. Subjective feedback was ubiquitously positive. The time costs to parents of involvement was very various in different projects, and this has implications for the wider involvement of more parents.

Conclusion

Overall, then, the research evidence suggests that maths games, cooperative learning in maths, peer tutoring in maths and parental involvement in maths can all be effective separately. The Paired Maths method seeks to blend selected elements of these approaches together into a robust and dynamic package.

Research evidence on Paired Maths

Formative evaluation: parent involvement at Level 1

The initial Level 1 Paired Maths pilot project was evaluated formatively, gathering a good deal of structured feedback from parent and teacher participants, conducting informal observations, and experimenting with various maths tests. Subsequently, a further four parental involvement projects, two with infant reception children (aged 4 to 5) and two with first year juniors (aged 7 to 8), were operated. These involved an increase in the number of games available and a reduction in the recommended time to spend doing Paired Maths.

Outcome evaluation: parent involvement at Level 1

In the second infant project, all the parents for the new intake for that term were invited to take part, 12 of the 16 parents accepting. The children in the next term's intake, who were not offered any project involvement, were used as a comparison group. The QUEST diagnostic tests (Robertson et al. 1983) were used with all the experimental children pre- and post-project, and with the comparison children over the same eight-week time interval.

The project children showed a marked improvement, particularly in the areas of pattern, order and conservation. The children in the comparison group, although showing some improvement in their scores, scored significantly less well than the project children, particularly in these same areas. Pre-project scores for project children were on average below those of the comparison children, but post-project this situation was reversed. For more details see Topping and Bamford (1998).

Projects at Level 2: qualitative evaluation

The greatest difference between the infant and junior projects was the ease of joint involvement for parents and teachers in the infant school in the exchange of games. In the infant school the parents were already visiting school to collect their children, but in the first junior school project the parents' main contact was through the home–school record card. In the second junior project this distancing was reduced by explicitly contracting for the parents to visit school weekly to exchange games with the children, and for the teachers to be available to discuss aspects of the games where necessary.

Evaluation of each of the projects involved not only the children but also the parents and the teachers. Parents were involved through discussion at meetings before and after the project, through discussion with teachers, and through the completion of record cards and questionnaire returns after the project. Teachers were involved through discussion at meetings and on other occasions during, before and after the project. Pupils were involved through parents' observations and questionnaire comments, observations by teachers, and tape-recorded discussions after the project.

The parents' reactions were very positive and suggested that they had found it easy to take part in the projects. The introduction and use of the mathematical language generally presented no problems. They reported that the children were sufficiently keen to play the games that they would remind their parents if they forgot, and only occasionally did either parents or children become bored with the activities. Many of the parents said that the games had given them ideas of other things to do at home and that they would continue to play games even after the project was finished. Both the parents and the teachers felt that the children's confidence in maths had increased, and both remarked upon the children's disappointment when the project ended.

Follow-up: extending and embedding parental involvement

Some time after the initial establishment of the Paired Maths approach, 17 schools were visited and interviews held with the head teachers and teachers involved in the continuing parental involvement in maths. All of the schools continued to rely on the subjective evaluation feedback given by the parents and children through their verbal and written comments and their continuing involvement in the project (see Sections B7 to B9).

Six of the schools had incorporated Paired Maths into their annual cycle of parental involvement alongside Paired Reading. The numbers of pupils generally involved included the whole year group, operating at different times during the year – extending to many hundreds of children in any one of the schools over a period of years. One of the schools with a large proportion of children for whom

English was not the home language had made Paired Maths their premier way of involving new pupils and their parents, who could use their home language to play the games and their contact through the language support tutors to explain to and encourage their children.

In each of the schools where the project was embedded, the organisation had become much more the responsibility of the parents themselves, although it is difficult to know whether this was cause or effect.

Outcome evaluation: peer tutoring

Detailed feedback from participants in a same-age peer Paired Maths Level 3 project involving parallel classes of 11 to 12-year-olds in a high school in a disadvantaged area was collated by Topping and Bamford (1990). The children considered the strategy box to be the most interesting. Three-dimensional commercially-produced games were preferred to two-dimensional locally-produced games. However, the instructions were considered too long and too hard for several games, especially the commercial ones. No participant became bored – a change of game easily avoided any such possibility. Discussion about how to play the game was commonly reported; pairs sometimes agreed to change the rules.

Overall, participants definitely found Paired Maths both interesting and fun. They felt a majority of the games made them think harder. However, they were unsure about whether they had increased their liking of 'maths' – although they certainly liked the maths games! A few participants felt they could do 'problems' better in formal maths classes, and there was spontaneous comment that needing to read complex instructions very carefully improved the ability to do this in other subjects. The vast majority of participants wished to go on doing Paired Maths. Verbatim comments included: 'it didn't feel like maths, because it was fun'.

A more substantial controlled evaluation of a Level 2 project was reported by Mallinson (see Chapter 6 in Topping and Bamford 1998). The experimental group was a mixed-ability class of 25 10-year-old children. The comparison group was a parallel class of 20 children, who did not play the games but received normal mathematical instruction from their teacher. The children played the games only for two 30-minute sessions each week for six weeks. Pairs were organised so that there was one child who could read well in each pair.

A criterion-referenced test was devised by the researcher which was appropriate for the age and ability range of the children. An attitude questionnaire was also devised by the researcher (see Section B10), which was read out to the children who marked their multiple-choice answer.

The attitude to maths scores of both groups did not show significant change. However, the experimental group had significantly higher self-esteem scores post-test than pre-test, while those of the comparison group were slightly lower. On the mathematics test, the experimental group scores increased significantly while those of the comparison group did not. Boys improved much more than girls. At pre-test the comparison group had scored significantly higher than the experimental group, but by post-test the experimental group had caught them up.

Conclusion

Overall, then, there is good evidence of the positive impact of Paired Maths at Levels 1 and 3 on maths attainment outcomes, and positive qualitative evaluation from Levels 1, 2 and 3.

Evaluating Paired Maths

We will not dwell here on issues of research design, which readers can explore elsewhere (e.g. Topping 1988), but focus on problems of assessment and measurement in mathematics, particularly with young children.

The most important question in evaluation is: what was the purpose or objective of the project – what was the desired outcome? It is unreasonable to expect one small project to change everything overnight, so set realistic targets. The next question concerns how you intend to measure whether the objectives or outcomes have been attained, and this will lead you to consider qualitative measures, quantitative measures, or both.

Especially if tests are to be used, the selection of a measuring instrument for quantitative outcome evaluation depends on the purposes underlying the project, and whether group or individual administration is practical. The age, range of ability, and level of attainment of the children also affect the choice of test. Norm-referenced, criterion-referenced or diagnostic tests can be used. Commercial normed group maths tests tend to be very wide-ranging and rather superficial and insensitive, as maths is such a vast subject and mathematical competence far from being a unitary skill. In addition to the discussion about research earlier in this section, more detailed information about suitable tests will be found in Topping and Bamford (1998).

Qualitative evaluation often relies on the subjective experiences of the people who are involved with the project. Evaluation insights can be gained through questionnaires and discussion. Questionnaires might need to be read out to weaker readers. Changes in attitudes can be measured either by scales and questionnaires or by open-ended discussion or by structured direct observation. Designing questionnaires is not easy, and care must be taken not to introduce bias. A sample of types of questionnaires that have been used by different groups of parents and pupils will be found in Sections B7 to B10.

Process data should also be gathered during the project, to indicate how smoothly the organisation is running. Diary/record cards yield weekly information which can be summarised.

If your evaluation outcomes seem disappointing, think carefully about why this might have been.

- Were your objectives too wide-ranging, or unrealistically high?
- Did you measure only the outcomes *you* wanted to see, forgetting that other key players might have had quite different objectives, which were not measured?
- Was the project organisation appropriate in principle, but just not properly implemented (for whatever reasons), so your results are not a fair test of the programme when properly implemented?

- Ask yourself about the measuring instruments used – were they relevant or sensitive enough?
- Was it that the programme design was perfectly appropriate for some cultural settings and contexts, but not really for the one in which you operate?

In short, poor outcome results might be the result of wrong objectives, wrong organisational planning, poor implementation, wrong measures, or some combination thereof. If you suffer from any of these, take steps to fix the problem.

Further development of Paired Maths

The Paired Maths structure offers many avenues for development. Some teachers start with parental involvement then try peer tutoring, while others develop it the other way round. Most start at a lower Level then try a higher one. Peer tutoring can start same-age then become cross-age, or vice versa. Some try Paired Maths then become interested in Paired Science (Topping 1998), others the other way round.

After becoming familiar with Paired Maths through projects with 'ordinary' mixed-ability children, teachers might feel confident to target a more challenging group, perhaps children with learning difficulties or particularly hard-to-reach parents. A cross-school reciprocal peer tutoring Paired Maths project involving special needs children with severe learning difficulties is described in Chapter 7 of Topping and Bamford (1998), for those seeking inspiration.

Beyond this, computer-based maths games and activities are increasingly available – and to promote cooperative interaction, not just play in isolation. In addition to software borrowed from libraries or purchased, the Internet is increasingly a source of such material, which can be downloaded or used online. Further details will be found in Topping and Bamford (1998). We are almost certainly moving into the era of 'Electronic Paired Maths', and 'Electronic Family Numeracy'. Nevertheless, there will always be a place for tangible games in three dimensions, and those playable with the simplest of everyday materials – a few stones and lines marked in the dust.

References

Britz, M. W. *et al.* (1989) 'The effects of peer tutoring on mathematics performance: a recent review', *B. C. Journal of Special Education* **13**(1), 17–33.

Brodsky, S. *et al.* (1994) *An Urban Family Math Collaborative.* New York: Center for Advanced Study in Education, City University of New York. Educational Resources Information Center, ED379154.

Cockcroft, W. H. (1982) *Mathematics Counts: Report of the Committee of Enquiry into the Teaching of Mathematics in Schools.* London: HMSO.

Cohen, P. A., Kulik, J. A., Kulik, C-L. C. (1982) 'Educational outcomes of tutoring: a meta-analysis of findings', *American Educational Research Journal* **19**(2), 237–48.

Davidson, N. (1985) 'Small group learning in mathematics', in Slavin, R. *et al.* (eds) *Learning to Cooperate, Cooperating to Learn.* New York: Plenum Press.

Davidson, N. (1989) 'Cooperative learning and mathematics achievement: a research review', *Cooperative Learning* **10**(2), 15–16.

Davidson, N. (ed.) (1990) *Cooperative Learning in Mathematics: A Handbook for Teachers.* Menlo

Park CA: Addison-Wesley.

Davidson, N. and Kroll, D. L. (1991) 'An overview of research on cooperative learning related to mathematics', *Journal for Research in Mathematics Education* **22**(5), 362–5.

Merttens, R. and Vass, J. (1987) 'Parents in schools: raising money or raising standards?' *Education 3–13*, June, 23–7.

Merttens, R. and Vass, J. (eds) (1993) *Partnerships in Maths: Parents and Schools – The IMPACT Project*. London and Washington DC: Falmer Press.

Nunes, T. and Bryant, P. (1996) *Children Doing Mathematics*. Oxford and Cambridge MA: Blackwell.

Robertson, A. H. *et al.* (1983) *Quest: Screening, Diagnostic and Remediation Kit*. Walton-on-Thames: Nelson.

Sharpley, A. M. and Sharpley, C. F. (1981) 'Peer tutoring: a review of the literature', *Collected Original Resources in Education (CORE)* **5**(3), 7–C11 (fiche 7 & 8).

Skemp, R. R. (1971) *The Psychology of Learning Mathematics*. Harmondsworth: Penguin.

Skemp, R. R. (1978) *Intelligence, Learning and Action*. Chichester: Wiley.

Skemp. R. R. (1989) *Mathematics in the Primary School*. London: Routledge.

Topping, K. J. (1988) *The Peer Tutoring Handbook: Promoting Co-operative Learning*. London: Croom Helm; Cambridge MA: Brookline.

Topping, K. J. (1995) *Paired Reading, Spelling and Writing: The Handbook for Teachers and Parents*. London and New York: Cassell.

Topping, K. J. (1998) *The Paired Science Handbook: Parental Involvement and Peer Tutoring in Science*. London: David Fulton Publishers; Bristol PA : Taylor & Francis.

Topping, K. J. and Wolfendale, S. W. (eds) (1985) *Parental Involvement in Children's Reading*. London: Croom Helm; New York: Nichols.

Topping, K. J. and Bamford, J. (1990) *Paired Maths at Deighton High School: Evaluative Feedback*. Huddersfield: Kirklees Psychological Service.

Topping, K. J. & Bamford, J. (1998) *Parental Involvement and Peer Tutoring in Mathematics and Science: Developing Paired Maths into Paired Science*. London: David Fulton Publishers; Bristol PA : Taylor & Francis.

Topping, K. J. and Ehly, S. (eds) (1998) *Peer Assisted Learning*. Mahwah NJ and London: Erlbaum.

Wolfendale, S. W. and Topping, K. J. (eds) (1996) *Family Involvement in Literacy: Effective Partnerships in Education*. London and New York: Cassell.

Section B:
Resources for Setting up Paired Maths (Reproducible)

Note: In Section B4, the top half of the first page is the diary side of the Diary and Language Card, and is the same on all cards. The rest of the section gives the different language to be used in each of the six different subsets of game types or boxes. Six different sets of cards should be produced, each a different colour to match the colour coding of each game type or box, each having the diary layout on one side and the specifically relevant language information on the back.

These specimen resources are not intended to be adhered to rigidly, and many schools will wish to develop their own version to suit their own context. For instance, the first Parents' Leaflet (B2) might be seen as simplistic and patronising in a socio-economically advantaged area. Equally, some of the sample questionnaires might appear too simple or too complex for particular applications.

ORGANISATIONAL CHECKLIST

For each item, specify person responsible and time deadline.
Tick box when item complete.

1 Briefing and planning
1.1 Date of meeting(s)? ☐
1.2 Present (head teacher, class teacher/s, others)? ☐

2 Games
2.1 Source of funding? ☐
2.2 Who orders games? ☐
2.3 Who checks/modifies instructions? ☐
2.4 Who packages and codes? ☐
2.5 Time allotted? ☐
2.6 Date games available? ☐

3 Other materials
3.1 Source of printing? ☐
3.2 Who orders leaflets? ☐
3.3 Who orders Diary/Language cards? ☐
3.4 Date printing available? ☐

4 Letters/invitations
4.1 Target children chosen? ☐
4.2 Who writes letters? ☐
4.3 Letter sent? ☐
4.4 Date of launch meeting? ☐

5 Launch meeting
5.1 Games available? ☐
5.2 Cards available? ☐
5.3 Booklet available? ☐
5.4 Loan chart made? ☐
5.5 Tea/coffee/creche available? ☐
5.6 Day/time/place for exchange fixed? ☐

6 Running project
6.1 Where are games stored/displayed? ☐
6.2 Who monitors game exchange? ☐
6.3 Who comments at foot of Diary Card? ☐
6.4 Where/how are Diary Cards stored? ☐
6.5 Who talks to parents and resolves any problems? ☐
6.6 Date of follow-up meeting? ☐

7 Post-project meeting
7.2 Who writes invite letter? ☐
7.3 Letter sent? ☐
7.4 Who orders questionnaire printing? ☐
7.5 Tea/coffee/creche available? ☐

8 Follow-up
8.1 Who circulates information? ☐
8.2 Who follows up with parents? ☐

9 Evaluation
9.1 Teacher or child questionnaires? ☐
9.2 Language or other mathematical assessment? ☐

'WHAT TO DO' PARENT LEAFLET

We are pleased that you have decided to help with your child's mathematical development. This project will last for six weeks. The meeting gave you details about what to do. These notes are to help you remember.

This is what you will have:

- a mathematical game
- a card with suggestions on how to play the game
- a Diary Record Card with useful words on the back.

This is what to do:

- Try to help your child to enjoy playing the games daily.
- Choose a time and place which are good for you.
- It would be best if you could be alone without distractions.
- You should spend about 10 minutes playing the game.
- Don't stop the game as long as it continues to be enjoyable.
- Do stop the game if it becomes boring or too difficult.

Things to remember:

- Make the time spent enjoyable for both of you.
- If your child makes a mistake do not make a fuss.
- Just tell him the correct answer or show her how to do it.
- Then go through it again.
- Let your child discover as much as possible without your help.
- Do encourage and guide if you feel this is needed.

Talk with your child – listen to your child

It is important that you and your child talk about what you are doing. Each Diary Card has a list of words you should try to use, but you may find some more words yourself.

Who should play the games?

If you are unable to play the games on any occasion please ensure that the person who takes over for you knows about the aims of the project.

Diary Record Card

We would like you to note down a few things for us each time you play the games with your child. Please return the Diary Record Card to school every week during the project.

'FURTHER HINTS' PARENT LEAFLET

You can help your child in many ways:

- Your child does not only learn in school.
- You were your child's first teacher.
- Children can be helped at home in many ways.
- A lot of these ways are easy and need not stop you getting on with other things you have to do.

Talking and listening

- Try to answer your child's questions and ask questions yourself about what your child is doing.
- Do things with your child and talk about them as you do them.
- Nursery rhymes, stories, jingles and number rhymes are important.
- Talk about pictures in books and magazines.

Watch children's television *with* your child and talk about it. Your child can talk to you but not to the television.

These things can help your child learn maths:
- different sizes of pans with lids to fit,
- plastic containers of all sizes and shapes,
- a box of assorted buttons,
- a collection of different sized empty boxes,
- old weights and scales,
- washing-up bowls, sieve, colander, squeezy bottles, funnel, and sponge,
- nails, screws, nuts, and bolts from the toolbox,
- old newspapers, magazines, contents of rag bag,
- different-sized pieces of wood.

In fact, almost anything in the home, used for a purpose and talked about will teach your child something.

What can it teach your child?

The following are two examples from the above list:

A set of pans
These can teach your child that:
- they are the same shape, that some will hold more when filled with liquid,
- one is bigger than another,
- there is a biggest one and a smallest one,
- only one lid will fit one particular pan,
- they can fill them with water, sand, soil, leaves, etc.

A collection of buttons

These can teach your child:

- different sizes, shapes, colours,
- that some have holes at the back, and some have holes through them,
- some are rough and some smooth, shiny, dull, patterned or not patterned.
- Let your child sort them into different piles and tell you which is the biggest pile, the smallest pile, or how many there are in a pile. Old margarine cartons could be used to hold the different piles.

What you do in the home will help your child to learn:

- Getting dressed – in a definite order, pairs of socks, how many buttons, matching buttons to buttonholes, etc.
- Time – the order of the day – breakfast time, dinner time, tea time, bedtime, time to go to school etc., words such as 'before' or 'after'.
- Laying the table – one thing for one person, cutting up the pie in equal parts or portions, small and large portions, different sizes of cups – which one holds the most?
- Cooking – measuring, weighing, cutting, playing with dough for pleasure, dividing up the dough.
- Helping – digging in the garden, washing the car, helping to do odd repair jobs – carrying things, wrapping things, explaining about length, weight, volume and capacity.
- Shopping – lots of possibilities for talking about quantity, weights, size, price, total costs.
- Playing in sand and water (including at bath time) – especially filling one container from another, seeing containers of different shapes can hold the same amount of water, etc.

These words are used in maths – use them at home as well!

big	more than	next	up
bigger	less than	heavy	down
biggest	more	light	high
too big	less	first	low
the same as	a lot	last	near
fast	tall	flat	not far
slow	long	round	nearly
on	short	thick	almost
off	full	thin	under
little	empty	too much	over
small	different	inside	on top of
before	few	outside	fewer
after	fill	in	most
how	out	straight	least

DIARY AND LANGUAGE CARDS

NAME:		
GAME:		BOX:
Day	How long?	Words/concepts used + comments
Monday		
Tuesday		
Wednesday		
Thursday		
Friday		
Saturday		
Sunday		
Teacher comment:		

Words to use with CONSERVATION	Words to use with MATCHING
long	smaller
short	bigger
too many	same
too few	different
more	exactly
same	nearly
exactly	almost
longer	most
less	least
different	more

Words to use with ORDER	Words to use with COUNTING
first	up
last	down
next	first
order	next
middle	again
most	more
least	straight
big	nearly
bigger	in
biggest	out

Words to use with PATTERN	Words to use with SHAPES
more than	same
more than	different
before	small
after	big
a lot	square
round	circle
the same as	triangle
different	complete
on top	nearly
under	more

MATHS GAMES BORROWED AND RETURNED

	Category and colour code of box				
Name of child	Put in number of game taken – tick on return				

CORE MATHEMATICAL VOCABULARY

big	more than	next	up
bigger	less than	heavy	down
biggest	more	light	high
too big	less	first	low
the same as	a lot	last	near
fast	tall	flat	not far
slow	long	round	nearly
on	short	thick	almost
off	full	thin	under
little	empty	too much	over
too small	float	inside	on top of
before	sink	outside	open
after	pour	in	closed
how	hot	out	straight
light	cold	wet	different
dark	few	dry	most
fewer	least		

PARENT EVALUATION QUESTIONNAIRE

Name of your child: _____

School: _____ Age of child: _____

Please circle the answer which is true for you, or put in your comment where asked:

1 I found it easy to take part in the project

      yes   no   not sure

2 I found the game instructions difficult to follow

      yes   no   not sure

3 I found using the maths words on the Diary Cards

      easy   difficult   not sure

4 My child sometimes reminded me if I forgot our daily session

      yes   no   I never forgot

5 I became bored with the daily sessions

      very soon   occasionally   not at all

6 My child became bored with the daily sessions

      very soon   occasionally   not at all

7 I will probably go on doing maths games with my child(ren)

      every day   regularly   only sometimes

8 Did you use any other maths games?

      yes   no

If yes, what did you do?

9 I have recommended Paired Maths to other parents

          yes   no

10 I will recommend Paired Maths to other parents

          yes   probably   not really

11 What did you and your child learn from the project?

12 Have you noticed any other changes in your child?

13 Do you have any suggestions for improvements:
(a) in instructions?

(b) in games?

(c) in organisation?

(d) in anything else?

14 Which games did you like best?

15 Any other comments?

THANK YOU VERY MUCH

TEACHER EVALUATION QUESTIONNAIRE

Please mark the response which best indicates the direction and strength of your view, and insert your other specific comments:

A Organisation

Involving the children with maths games was:

Enjoyable	1	2	3	4	5	Not very enjoyable
Interesting	1	2	3	4	5	Not very interesting
Hard work	1	2	3	4	5	Easy
Useful	1	2	3	4	5	Not very useful
Difficult to organise	1	2	3	4	5	Easy to organise

Comments:

B Observation of children's involvement

	Majority	Some	Few
Improved cooperation with partner	☐	☐	☐
Increased discussion of tasks	☐	☐	☐
Increased interest and enthusiasm	☐	☐	☐
Increased concentration span	☐	☐	☐
Improved attitude to maths	☐	☐	☐

Comments:

C General

1 What did you feel were the major benefits of the project?

2 What were the most obvious drawbacks?

3 How could the project be improved?

Final comment (have we missed anything?):

EXTENDED JOINT EVALUATION QUESTIONNAIRE

What do you think?

Please circle the answer you think is right for you or put in your ideas where asked:

1 Which games did you like best?

2 Was one box of games especially:
   (a) boring?   (yes or no)   which box? ....
   (b) interesting? (yes or no)   which box? ....

3 Were there too many games, enough or not enough?
         too many   enough   not enough

4 Was it hard or easy to choose good games?
         hard   easy

5 Were the rules and instructions too long or too hard for some games?
     no   yes for a   yes for a lot   yes for most
                  few games

6 Was it easy or hard to sort out which partner did what?
     easy   hard   varied

7 Did you get bored?
     no   a bit   a lot

8 Did your partner(s) get bored?
     no   a bit   a lot

9 Did you *talk* about the games?
     no   a bit   a lot

10 Did you change the rules of any games?
     yes   no

11 Do you now get on with your partner(s):
     better   worse   the same

12 Overall, was Paired Maths: (a) fun?   yes   no
                           (b) interesting?   no   yes

13 Did Paired Maths: (a) make you think?   yes   no
                                (b) help you learn maths?   no   yes

14 Are you now better at: (a) maths games?   yes   no
                                (b) all kinds of maths?   no   yes

15 Do you like maths more now?   yes   no

16 Do you put more maths mistakes right by yourself now?   no   yes

17 Could you find or invent some maths games of your own?   yes   no

18 Did any other good things come out of doing Paired Maths?

19 Would you recommend Paired Maths to others?   no   yes

20 How could we make Paired Maths better?

21 Do you want to: (a) stop Paired Maths for now?
    (choose only one)   (b) go on, but only twice a week?
                             (c) go on as often as before?
                             (d) do other maths work in pairs?

22 Any other comments?

THANK YOU FOR TELLING US WHAT YOU THINK

Name: _____

'FEELINGS' QUESTIONNAIRE FOR PAIRED MATHS WITH PEERS

How do you feel about it?

Write your name here_____

Below are 16 statements about maths, school work, how you feel about your work and about working with other children.

Please circle one answer which best shows what *you* think. There are no 'right' answers.

Please circle your answer

1	I enjoy maths lessons	Yes	Sometimes	Not really	No
2	I have lots of friends	Yes	Sometimes	Not really	No
3	My teacher thinks my work could be better	Yes	Sometimes	Not really	No
4	I like to keep my ideas to myself	Yes	Sometimes	Not really	No
5	Maths games are boring	Yes	Sometimes	Not really	No
6	I try my hardest in maths	Yes	Sometimes	Not really	No
7	Working with a partner is stupid	Yes	Sometimes	Not really	No
8	Some days I don't care if I do bad work	Yes	Sometimes	Not really	No
9	Maths is a hard subject	Yes	Sometimes	Not really	No
10	You can solve problems with a partner	Yes	Sometimes	Not really	No
11	My work is quite bad	Yes	Sometimes	Not really	No
12	I can understand maths words	Yes	Sometimes	Not really	No
13	Other children don't like to work with me	Yes	Sometimes	Not really	No
14	The others think I am 'ace' at maths	Yes	Sometimes	Not really	No
15	I work well with a partner	Yes	Sometimes	Not really	No
16	It's good to help others in lessons	Yes	Sometimes	Not really	No

NATIONAL CURRICULUM LINKAGE, LEVEL 1

Statement of Attainment

Paired Maths directly helps children achieve the following (example of relevant game in brackets):

- use materials provided for a task

- talk about own work and ask questions

- make predictions based on experience (e.g. Rods)

- count and order numbers to at least 10

- know that size of a set = the last number in the count

- understand the conservation of number (e.g. Scaredy Cat)

- add/subtract using objects, numbers no greater than 10 (e.g. Buttons)
- copy, continue and devise repeating patterns represented by objects/apparatus (e.g. Mosaics)
- compare and order objects without measuring, and use appropriate language (e.g. Old Woman)

- sort two-dimensional shapes (e.g. Tangrams)

- recognise squares, rectangles, circles, triangles, hexagons (e.g. Mr Shape)

- state a position using prepositions (e.g. Jigsaws)

- select criteria for sorting a set of objects and apply consistently (e.g. Buttons)

- recognise possible outcomes of simple random events (e.g. Snakes and Ladders)

NATIONAL CURRICULUM LINKAGE, LEVEL 3

A typical Level 3 games kit might have up to 200 games and puzzles, divided into five categories:
1. Number Games,
2. Space Games,
3. Strategy Games,
4. Solitaire or Cooperative Puzzles, and
5. Extension Games and Puzzles.

Of course, not all areas of the maths National Curriculum are approachable through games, while games also develop aspects not specifically part of the National Curriculum. Nevertheless, there is close correlation in many areas. For example . . .

Paired Maths directly helps children achieve:

Application Level 3/4: Select relevant maths, predict outcome, check results plausible, record (e.g. Equality, Casino, Number Grids, Guess My Number, What's My Rule?)

Number Level 3/4: Read, write, order and understand numbers (not decimals, fractions, percentages) (e.g. Checkmath, Shut the Box, Multichance, Calculator Tricks)

Number Level 3/4: Add and subtract mentally two two-digit numbers (e.g. Rithmomachia, Little Professor)

Number Level 4: Estimate, approximate, use 'trial and improvement' method (e.g. Clash, Congclak)

Algebra Level 4/5: Strategically explore number properties, spatial patterns, sequences and rules (e.g. 36 Square, Shuttles, Counterfeat, most Strategy games)

Algebra Level 3: Understand unknown numbers and simple functions (e.g. Number Quest, Martian Maths)

Measures Level 4: Estimate measures of everyday objects and events (e.g. Detective)

Shape Level 3/4: Sort and construct two- and three-dimensional shapes (e.g. Enigma, Labyrinth, Action Replay)

Space Level 4/5: Use coordinates for location and identify symmetry (e.g. Navigrid, Distort)

Data use Level 3/4: Collect, group and order discrete data (e.g. Pit, Yahtzee, Packing, Relations)

Data use Level 4: Understand and estimate probability of outcomes (e.g. Greed, Devil's Triangle)

Section C:
Reproducible Mathematical Games

Reproducible Mathematical Games

User notes

This section includes a number of game boards and instructions for 76 mathematical games which can be played with counters, dice, sticks, paper and pencil or other simple materials. Game boards and rules are printed separately. Note that some games do not have boards, only instructions, and that sometimes more than one game can be played on the same board. Instructions are written in clear, simple, low readability language (although 'die' is used as the correct singular of 'dice', and 'diagonally' might need explaining). In the instructions, the word 'counter' has been used to mean 'playing piece', as plastic counters are cheap and convenient for this purpose. However, players can use pebbles, seed pods, buttons, or even small sweets (candies), provided they are small enough for the size of board – some players like to use their own personal 'lucky' pieces.

The expectation is that users will create enlarged photocopies of the game boards, mount these on card and cover them with clear plastic laminate for durability. The instructions should be similarly enlarged and laminated. You can make a separate set of instructions for each player if you wish. It is then helpful to keep game board, rules and any required materials (e.g. counters, dice) in a resealable plastic bag. Parent or pupil volunteers can easily help with this.

The games are a mixture of ancient and modern public domain items. The main orientation of these two-dimensional games is to children aged 9 to 12, since younger children especially benefit from three-dimensional games. However, it is stressed that Paired Maths with older children should still include some three-dimensional games, which even older children find highly motivating.

The game boards are in five conceptual areas of mathematics (Strategy, Space, Number, Puzzles, Extension), indicated by codes (St, Sp, Nu, Pu and Ex). Those which come with a reproducible game board also have a B in the code to indicate this. Within these categories, each separate game then has its own number. Some card games (CG) and card solitaire puzzles (CS) requiring only a pack of playing cards complete the collection – many of these are strongly number-oriented.

For ease of use, the games should also be colour-coded by area (e.g. St = yellow, Sp = red, Nu = green, Pu = blue, Ex = orange) and kept in a box marked with the same colour.

Some of the instructions are deliberately designed to encourage players to think about the structure of the game with a view to designing alternative rules or game boards. Some players may design completely new games, and this design and subsequent field-testing process presents challenges of great educational value.

However, it is assumed that where the games are used in a peer tutoring context the supervising teacher will be circulating to monitor any difficulties with understanding, accuracy, relationships or honesty, and also to encourage discussion, analysis, and the further development of games, perhaps into wider mathematical investigations. Where the games are used at home, parents are encouraged to do likewise insofar as they are able. Guard against requiring much written recording – it rapidly becomes tedious and demotivating. The thinking is what is important – recording is only useful if it enhances thinking.

As they experience the different types of game in this collection, players may educe some of the abstract principles of game design. For instance, particularly with reference to Strategy and Space Games, often one or more of the following principles are involved:

- trapping, blocking or sandwiching opposing pieces,
- eliminating or 'taking' opposing pieces off the board (often by jumping),
- line games (form a line or mill to win),
- race or journey games (to an endpoint or back to base),
- exchange of position of opposing pieces,
- insertion of pieces (one at a time),
- extraction or pick-up of pieces,
- riddance – first to get rid of their pieces wins,
- distribution of pieces among locations.

These and other principles can then be explicitly and actively deployed when designing new games.

INSTRUCTIONS FOR STRATEGY GAMES WITH GAME BOARDS

GO   (StB1)

You need: game board, 50 counters of one colour, 50 of another.

This is the most popular board game in Japan. It is sometimes played by professionals who earn a lot of money at it. This version is simpler, sometimes known as 'Spoil Five', and arrived in the UK around 1885.

You can play it either on the squares of the board, or on the points where lines cross. Take turns to put one of your counters on the board. Aim to make a row of five of your counters in any direction, including diagonally. The winner is the first to do this.

MATCHING MIN   (StB2)

You need: game board, 12 counters of one colour, 12 of another.

The aim is to be the first player to get rid of all your counters. Player A puts 1, 2, 3, 4 or 5 counters in the first circle (see arrow). Player B must put the *same* number in the opposite circle.

Player B then puts 1, 2, 3, 4 or 5 counters in the next circle, and Player A has to match them. And so on, taking turns.

PALM TREE   (StB3)

You need: game board, 5 counters of one colour, 5 of another, one die.

This game comes from ancient Egypt. A playing board was found in the tomb of the Pharaoh Amenemhet the Fourth, who lived about 3,800 years ago.

Each player starts from the sun. Take turns to roll the die to see how many spaces you must go. But if you roll 4 or 6, you don't count the score, but you can roll the die again. If you throw 5 you *do* count the score *and* you get another go.

Race from the sun around the board and up to the top five positions up the palm tree. Each player goes round their own side of the board.

The connecting lines are like Snakes and Ladders – if you land on them exactly you must go along the line. If you land exactly on a hole marked with a cross, you can send any enemy counter back to the start, except for those already at the top of the tree.

You can see that this game is a bit like our modern Ludo. Can you make it more exciting by agreeing to change the rules in some way?

SEEGA   (StB4)

You need: game board, 12 counters of one colour, 12 of another.

This very old game comes from Egypt. Take turns to put two counters at a time on any squares except the centre one.

After putting all the counters on the board, take turns to move any one of your counters one square (*not* diagonally).

If you can sandwich an enemy counter between two of yours, you take it off the board and get another move. A counter on the centre square is safe and cannot be taken. You can move between two enemy counters yourself without being taken. If the other player cannot go, you must move again.

When you get to the point where no more counters can be taken, the player with most counters left is the winner.

LUDUS LATRUNCULORUM is a more complicated version of this game.

LUDUS LATRUNCULORUM (StB5)

You need: the game board for SEEGA, 16 counters of one colour plus a special big or marked counter called the Dux, same of another colour for the other player.

This game was popular with Roman soldiers. Take turns to place two counters at each turn on any squares except the middle one. Your Dux must be placed on the board last. Once all the counters are on the board, take turns to move one of your counters one square up, down or across but not diagonally.

If you sandwich an enemy counter between two of yours, you take it off the board and get another move. Any counter in the centre square cannot be taken. You are safe if you *move* between two enemy counters. If the other player can't go, you must go again. The Dux can also *jump over* any other single counter, but can be sandwiched just like an ordinary counter.

When it seems impossible for anyone to take any more pieces, the player with most counters left is the winner.

PATOLLI (StB6)

You need: game board, 6 counters of one colour, 6 of another, one die.

Patolli is the Aztec word for beans, which are still often used as pieces when this game is played in what is now Mexico.

Start at the one of the four centre squares which is nearest to you – this is your base. Each player can choose which way round the board they want to go. The aim is to have each of your counters travel right round the board, back to base and off. After the first counter, your other five counters can only start if you throw a 1 or a 6 on the die.

If you land on a curved end 'square' you get another go. Every counter must reach base with the exact number of squares thrown on the die. You can use a score of 6 on the die to move two counters any number of squares together adding up to 6.

You can choose either to agree that only one counter is allowed on any one square, or that if a counter is hit it must go back to base and start again. You can also choose to allow counters from one player to double up on one square, but then they can both be hit at the same time.

KONO (StB7)

You need: game board, 7 counters of one colour, 7 of another.

Start with Player A's counters on the points marked A, Player B's counters on the points marked B. Take turns to move one of your counters one space diagonally. Aim to end up in the other player's starting positions. First one there wins. There are no jumps or captures.

If you want a quicker game, agree to jumps (without taking the counter jumped over off the board) or chain jumps.

KUNGSER   (StB8)

You need: game board, 2 counters of one colour, and 24 of another.

This game comes from Tibet. It is a battle between two Princes and 24 Lamas (holy men). On the board, the starting places for the Princes is shown by an X, and those for the first eight Lamas by a black spot.

The first player can move a Prince one space, or capture a Lama by jumping over him to the space just on the other side. The second player uses every turn to put another Lama on the board until all 24 have been placed. After that, a move is one space.

Lamas try to win by trapping the Princes so they can't move.

Princes try to win by capturing Lamas until there are only eight left.

Lamas can try to force the Prince to capture one of them if it helps to trap the Prince. Chain captures, like in draughts, are allowed, so long as there is no break in the chain and there is an empty space to land for each part of the jump.

THE REBEL   (StB9)

You need: game board, 1 counter of one colour, and 16 of another.

This is a game from China. Sixteen soldiers try to catch the Rebel, who starts in his or her stronghold (castle). The soldiers start on the black squares. Soldiers can go anywhere except in the stronghold or the mountains, but the Rebel can go anywhere at all. Take turns to move a counter one space along a link in any direction.

The Rebel can kill two soldiers by moving into a space in a line between them – then the soldiers are taken off the board. Soldiers try to move so that *they* trap the Rebel between two soldiers, or block the Rebel in so he or she can't move at all.

CHINESE CHECKERS   (StB10)

You need: game board, 6 counters of one colour, 6 of another.

Player X puts their counters on the points marked X to start; Player O puts theirs on the points marked O.

The aim is to move your pieces to take up the other player's starting places. You take turns to move one space at a time to an empty space. You can jump over any other counter in a straight line, but jumped pieces are not taken off the board.

INSTRUCTIONS FOR SPACE GAMES WITH GAME BOARDS

ALQUERQUE   (SpB1)

You need: game board, 12 counters of your own colour each.

This game was found in the Temple of Kurna in Egypt, and is at least 3,500 years old. It was later brought from Africa to Spain by the Moors.

Player A and Player B put their counters on the board in the spaces marked A and B, then take turns to move one space along a link.

The aim is to capture counters by jumping over them to a space just on the other side, like in draughts. Chain jumps are allowed in a turn, so long as there is no break in the chain and there is an empty space to land for each part of the jump. If you *can* capture a piece you have to do it. You lose if you have no counters left, or if all moves are blocked. (You can also play without allowing backwards moves, to make it harder.)

FOX AND GEESE   (SpB2)

You need: game board, 1 counter of one colour, and 13 of another.

This is a Viking game – this version came from Iceland, where it is called Halatafl. Put the 13 counters (geese) on the board on the points 1 to 13. The fox can then go on any point it likes.

Geese have the first move. Moves are along a line to the next point which has no counter on it. The fox can kill a goose by jumping over it to a next point with no counter on it. No chain jumps are allowed in one turn. The geese win if they trap the fox so it can't move, but lose if the fox kills so many geese that they can never trap it. (You can make it harder by not allowing the geese to move backwards – sometimes this is played with 17 geese.)

HASAMI SHOGI   (SpB3)

You need: game board, 18 counters of one colour, 18 of another.

This game comes from Japan. Each player starts with all their pieces on the board, on the two rows nearest to them. The aim is to get five of your pieces in a straight line (not diagonally). In one turn you can move one counter any number of squares in rows or columns, but not diagonally. You cannot include your own two home-starting rows in your line of five.

You can also play another game on this board, where you start with an empty board and take turns to put your counters on it. The aim is *not* to complete a square (having your counters at every corner of a square). Whoever completes a square loses.

MAZES   (SpB4)

You need: enlarged photocopies of game board, paper and pencil each.

There are many different kinds of mazes. In the second and third on your game board, there is only one way in and you have to find the one way out. But in the first, there are a few ways in but many of them are dead ends – and the aim is to get to the treasure in the middle and then get out again the same way. Take turns or work together to find your way through all three mazes.

Now working on your own, invent a different kind of maze. Swap the mazes you have invented and see if your partner can do it. You could end up making many different mazes for other people to enjoy. You could also have maze races – see who can get through in the shortest time.

PATHWAY   (SpB5)

You need: game board, 12 counters of one colour, 12 of another.

Take turns to put one counter in any empty circle. Aim to make a path of your own counters which joins any side of the board to the opposite side; the winner is the first to do this. Your pathway can be of any shape, but it must be made of your counters in circles which touch each other.

If after all the counters have been put on the board there is still no path, then the players carry on taking turns by sliding any one of their counters into an empty circle just next to it.

AVOID   (SpB6)

You need: game board, about 15 counters of one colour, 15 of another.

Take turns putting one counter into any empty space on the board. But you *can't* put a counter in any space *next to* a space which already has a counter in it. The player who makes the last possible move is the winner.

Now see if you can make your own harder game board.

TRIADS   (SpB7)

You need: game board, 36 counters.

Put a counter on every point. Players take turns to pick up three counters at a time. Each of the three picked up *must* be on a corner of a triangle – but the triangle can be of any size. When you can't find a complete set of 3 to pick up like this, you have lost.

SZ'KWA   (SpB8)

You need: game board, 20 counters of one colour, 20 of another.

Take turns to put one counter on any empty space. The aim is to trap the other player's counters, by surrounding them and blocking them in so they can't move. When you trap a counter, take it off the board. You are allowed to trap more than one of the other player's counters in one turn.

When a player has no more counters left to put on the board, or no space is left where a counter can be placed without putting itself right into a trap, the game ends. Then the winner is the player who has trapped the most counters.

PENTOMINOS   (SpB9)

You need: game board, photocopy of game board (or tracing paper), scissors.

Cut out a set of playing pieces from the photocopy or tracing of the game board. Shuffle the pieces on the table. Share the pieces in turn between you. Take turns to place the pieces on the grid. Pieces cannot overlap. The last player able to make a move is the winner. No trying out the game by yourself in secret before you play it! Have at least one turn each at starting the game, to see if the first player to put a piece down is likely to do better.

Is it *possible* to place all the pieces on the board? Can you make other games – perhaps with pieces containing three or four or six squares?

QUADS   (SpB10)

You need: game board, 4 different colours of card, scissors.

Make four sets of four playing pieces in the four different colours of card, as on the game board.

One player plays 'colours' and the other plays 'shapes'. The colour player starts and puts any piece on any point. The shape player then has their turn, and so on. Once a piece is put on the board it cannot be moved, and the game ends when the last piece is placed.

The aim is to score points by forming 'quads' (a 2 x 2 block of pieces of your own kind) and 'rows' (a line of four pieces of your own kind – up, across or diagonal).

When scoring, a piece can be in any number of quads or rows and count for colour and shape (but the colour player can only score for colour and the shape player can only score for shape). Score two points for each quad of four different colours or shapes, 10 points for each quad all of the same colour or shape, three points for each row of four different colours or shapes, five points for each row all of the same colour or shape.

Agree on a total number of points to score to be the winner, and perhaps a number of games to win to be the overall winner. You can also play this game using the Ace, Jack, Queen and King from an ordinary pack of playing cards and imagine the board on the table or floor.

INSTRUCTIONS FOR NUMBER GAMES WITH GAME BOARDS

COMBINATIONS   (NuB1)

You need: game board, 2 dice, 12 counters of one colour, 12 of another.

Decide who goes first. On your turn, roll both dice. Add up the numbers you rolled. Use counters to cover that number on your game board – or cover any other numbers that add up to exactly the same amount. For example, if you rolled 5 and 3, adding up to 8, you could cover 8, 7 and 1, 6 and 2, 5 and 3, or 4 and 4.

Keep playing until neither of you can cover numbers that add up to what you roll on the dice. Add up the numbers which have not been covered on your board. The winner is the one with the lowest score. (This game is similar to the game you can buy known as Shut the Box.)

SIDEWINDER   (NuB2)

You need: game board, one counter.

The first player says a (fairly big) number – the 'target' number. The second player puts a counter on any number on the board and says that number.

The first player slides the same counter along a line in any direction to another number. This is added to the first number and the player says what the total is.

The second player slides to another number, adds it on, and says the new total. You must make a move and numbers can't be jumped.

The winner is the one who moves to make the total exactly equal to the target number. If you make the total go over the target number, you lose.

INSTRUCTIONS FOR PUZZLE GAMES
WITH GAME BOARDS

SOLITAIRE   (PuB1)

You need: the game board for Fox and Geese, 32 counters.

Put a counter on every point on the board except the centre one. Remove counters by jumping over them to the next empty point. Aim to remove all the counters except one, which should end up in the centre hole.

SHUNT   (PuB2)

You need: game board, 4 counters of one colour and 4 of another.

Put the four counters of one colour on squares 1 to 4, and the four counters of the other colour on squares 9 to 12. By moving counters along the track and using the sidings, try to change over all the counters, so the colours are in the opposite spaces from when you started. Only ever one counter per square. Try to take as few moves as possible. Once you have practised, you could record your moves and try to work out the best and quickest way of doing it.

ALL CHANGE   (PuB3)

You need: game board, 3 counters of one colour, 3 of another.

Put the counters of one colour on squares 2 to 4, the counters of the other colour on squares 5 to 6. Aim to change round the positions of the counters of different colour in as few moves as possible. You can move one square in any direction at a time, including diagonally, but every turn you must move a counter of the other colour to the turn before.

PENTALPHA   (PuB4)

You need: game board, 9 counters.

The aim is to place all nine counters on the board. But you can only do this in a special way. You must put the counter on an empty square, slide it to another square (which can be full or empty), and then to a third empty square – *and these three empty squares must be in a straight line.*

You can also use this board with nine counters to play a kind of Solitaire – see rules for Solitaire.

TREBLE INTERCHANGE   (PuB5)

You need: game board, 3 counters of one colour, 3 counters of another colour, one counter of a third colour.

Put the single coloured counter in the middle, three counters of one colour at one end and the 3 of the other colour at the other end.

Aim to have the two sets of three counters change places, ending with the single coloured counter back in the middle. You move first one of the three coloured counters, then the single counter, then one of the three of the other colour, and so on. You can only move one space along a straight line at a time, and then only if the space you move to is empty.

STICK AT IT   (PuB6)

You need: game board, 20 matchsticks.
Follow instructions on game board.

MARVELLOUS 26   (PuB7)

You need: game board, 12 counters or small pieces of card with the numbers 1 to 12 marked on them.

Counters must be put on the board to make 'runs' adding up to 26. The counters adding to 26 must be next to each other – you can't leave one out or jump over one when adding. The runs must be in straight lines or form an angle or other geometric shape.

To start with you will probably try to make runs along the sides of the two big triangles. When you get really good, you might be able to make all six long sides add up to 26. Can you make the central hexagon add up to 26 as well?

MAGIC TRIANGLES   (PuB8)

You need: game board to copy, paper, pencil.
A. Can you place the numbers 1 2 3 4 5 6 in the boxes so that the three numbers on each side of the triangle add up to the same total?
    You will want to make your tries on a separate piece of paper, or make little squares of paper with the numbers on that you can move around. There are four different ways of doing it – can you find them all? (Clue to start – try putting the 2 at the top and the 5 in the middle at the bottom.)
B. Now try it with more numbers!
    Try placing the numbers 0 to 9 so that the four numbers on each side add up to the same amount. How many different ways to do it can you find? Now try covering up one of the bottom boxes and using only the numbers 1 to 9. Make each side add up to 20.
C. Now use the numbers 1 to 10 so each side of the pentagon adds up to the same total. How many different ways are there? (There are at least three!)

OLD FARMER PUZZLE   (PuB9)

You need: game board, tracing paper and scissors.

The old farmer is retiring, and he has decided to share his land and property equally between his two sons and two daughters. The map of his estate is on the game board.

Can you divide the large square area into four parts which are exactly the same in size and shape, so that each part includes one house, one well and one tree?

You will need to trace over the map on the game board, and experiment with your tracing.

INSTRUCTIONS FOR EXTENSION GAMES WITH GAME BOARDS

MANCALA – WARI   (ExB1)

You need: Mancala game board, 48 counters.

There are many different Mancala games. They were first known in Egypt, and are now played all over Africa and have spread to Asia and the Americas. This one is called Wari (also see Congclak).

Each player plays in the six pits (spaces) on their side of the board. Start with four counters in every pit. The first player lifts *all* the counters from any one of their own pits, and 'sows' them, one counter into each of the next 4 pits, going anti-clockwise. The other player does the same, starting from any of their pits. You take turns like this. In any go, if the last counter is 'sowed' in an enemy's pit *and makes the total in that pit up to two or three*, you capture those counters and they go in your store. *And*, if any enemy pits *before* that pit had two or three counters in them, you capture those counters as well.

If you pick up 12 counters from a pit, you will be able to go right round the board, so miss out the pit you started from when you come back to it. The game ends when eight counters or less are left on the board, and each player takes half of these for their store. The player with most counters in their store wins. Or, if you are playing again, you can agree that the winner of each round scores points equal to the difference between their number of counters left and those of the loser.

MANCALA – CONGCLAK (ExB2)

You need: Mancala game board, 50 counters.

There are many different Mancala games. They were first known in Egypt, and are now played all over Africa and have spread to Asia and the Americas. This one is called Congclak (also see Wari).

Start with five counters in every hole. Take turns to play. Pick up any number of counters from one pit on your side of the board and 'sow' them, one in each of the next holes going around the board clockwise (going on to the other player's side of the board, and including your own store but not the other player's store).

If your last counter is sown in a loaded pit, you pick up the counters from that pit and carry on round sowing. If your last counter is sown in an empty pit on the other player's side of the board, the turn ends.

If your last sown counter falls in an empty pit on your own side, then the counters in the other player's pit opposite (if any) are captured and put in your store. If your last sown counter falls in a store, the turn ends.

The game ends when one player has no counters left in pits on their side. The other player then takes all the counters left on the board into their own store. The winner is the player with most counters in their store. You can also make a board with more or fewer pits, and there are versions with more than two rows of pits.

TABULA (ExB3)

You need: game board, 3 dice, 15 counters of one colour, 15 of another.

Each player has 15 counters to race round the track, from 'Start' to 'Home'. All counters enter the track at the start and move in the same direction.

On your go, throw all three dice together. You can move one, two or three of your counters up to the total value on the dice added together. For example, if you throw 3, 4 and 5 on the dice, you could:

(a) move one counter 12 spaces; or
(b) move two counters by 7 and 5, or 8 and 4, or 3 and 9; or
(c) move three counters by three, four and five spaces.

The winner is the first player to have all 15 counters 'Home'. Usually you have to arrive 'Home' exactly, but you might agree to ignore this rule.

RITHMOMACHIA (ExB4)

You need: game board, playing pieces for each player in the form of rounds, triangles, squares and a pyramid.

This game was played in the eleventh century. One player has white pieces (or 'evens') and the other player black pieces (or 'odds'). Each piece has a different number value (see game board). The pyramids are made up of a pile of other separate pieces – rounds, triangles and squares. (For white, the pyramid is 91 = 1 + 4 + 9 + 16 + 25 + 36, i.e. two rounds, two triangles and two squares. For black, 190 = 16 + 25 + 36 + 49 + 64, i.e. one round, two triangles and two squares.)

The games starts with the pieces set up as shown on the game board. Players take turns to move one piece at a time. A round can move to an empty space right next to it. A triangle can move three empty spaces in any direction. A square can move four empty spaces in any direction. A pyramid can move the same way as any of the pieces in it.

The aim is to capture the other player's pieces. You can do this in four ways:

1. by landing on a square which has an enemy piece on it,
2. by moving so that the number value of your piece multiplied by the number of empty squares between it and the enemy piece is equal to the number value of the enemy piece,
3. by moving pieces to either side of an enemy piece so that the number value of your surrounding pieces added together is equal to the number value of the enemy piece,
4. by surrounding the enemy piece on all four sides.

You should agree before you start on how to decide who has won. What you decide will depend on how much time you have to play, and on how good you are at the game. Common agreements are:

- the game ends when one player has captured a set number of enemy pieces (e.g. 15), or
- the game ends when one player has captured pieces to a set total number value (e.g. 160), or
- to set the total number value with a set number of pieces, or
- to set the total number value with a set number of digits on the pieces, or
- a combination of these.

Once you are good at the game, you might want to try more complicated agreements:

- at least three pieces taken to include an arithmetic progression (so each number is a fixed amount bigger than the one before, e.g. 3, 5, 7, 9), or
- at least three pieces taken to include a geometric progression (so each number is a fixed multiple of the one before, e.g. 2, 4, 6, 8), or
- at least three pieces taken to include a harmonic progression (so the reciprocals of each number are in arithmetic progression, e.g. 3, 4, 6, 12 – you might need to ask your teacher to explain reciprocals), or
- one of these but with more than three pieces, or
- some combination of these.

You can also change the size of the board, number of pieces, and number value of pieces if you wish – the possibilities are endless.

LATINO (ExB5)

You need: 2 photocopies (or hand-drawn copies) each of the game board, pencil and paper each.

Each player secretly makes up and writes in their own 8 x 8 Latin Square on one of their empty photocopies. In a Latin Square, each column and each row contains one (and only one) of the numbers 1, 2, 3, 4, 5, 6, 7, and 8 (in any order you like in each row and column).

Take turns to ask about the other player's square. You can ask for the total of any two or three numbers next to each other in a row or column, by using the coordinates on the grid (i.e. the bottom left hand square is A1, the top right hand is H8). If you ask about E5, E6 and E7, for instance, the other player must tell you the total from adding the numbers in those three squares together.

When one player is sure they know exactly what all the other player's square looks like, and has it written in on their other photocopy, the game ends. Show each other what you think the other player's square looks like. The one with most correct wins.

To make this game easier, use a smaller board (e.g. 6 x 6 and the numbers 1 to 6).

RAYBOX (ExB6)

You need: 2 photocopies each of the game board, paper and pencil each.

Each player secretly chooses a triangle on one copy of the board, and marks on all three sides (by a heavier line) a 'mirror' facing out. The second player tries to find out where the secret mirror triangle is, by sending a ray of light into the box and being told where it has come out of the box (in direction 1a or 1b, for instance). The aim is to find out exactly which triangle has the mirror, in as few guesses as possible. Remember rays of light bounce off flat mirrors at exactly the same angle as they hit them. You will want to use your other photocopy to keep track of your tries and the results. Now change over so the first player tries to guess where the second player has hidden their mirror on their photocopy.

When you are good at this, try the game with more mirror triangles. This can get very complicated very quickly, because one ray might bounce off a number of triangles in different ways before it comes out of the box.

LAP (ExB7)

You need: 2 photocopies each of the game board for Latino, paper and pencil each.

Each player divides their photocopied grid into four parts with heavier lines (and only four parts, with nothing left over). Each part must contain 16 of the small squares, but the parts will probably look quite different in every other way. Each part is given a letter (A, B, C, D).

In turn each player asks for information about four small squares on the other player's sheet at a time, by the grid coordinates. For example, asking about the four squares F, G, 3, 4 might get the answer: Three are in part C and one in part A. You will want to use your other photocopy to keep track of your tries and the results.

As soon as you think you know what the other player's sheet looks like, challenge to see it. But remember you have to be exactly right, or you lose! If you both decide to challenge at the same time, the one with most correct wins.

ENTROPY (ExB8)

You need: game board, 25 counters – 5 of each of 5 different colours.

One player is called the 'Experimenter' (E), and the other is the 'Universe' (U), who is good at *not* doing what E wants. There are six rounds of play. In the first round, U chooses any five counters and E puts them wherever E likes in empty spaces on the board. U can then slide any two counters up or down (but not diagonally and no jumping is allowed) into new places. In the second round and after, only four counters are chosen at a time. In the sixth round, all the squares will now be full, so U can make no slides.

The aim for E is to try to make the pattern at the end of the sixth round as orderly and symmetrical as possible, while U is trying to stop that. (You might need to ask your teacher what 'symmetrical' means.)

In each row or column, for every two counters in a symmetrical pattern, E scores two points, for every three symmetrical three points, and so on. You can use the same counter to be part of different scores. For instance, red would score two points and red–white–red would score three points, while in red–green–green–green–blue, the red and blue are not symmetrical and would score nothing, but the first two greens would score two, the last two greens would score two, and the three greens would score three, making a total of seven.

After one round, the players change places and the new E tries to beat the old one's score.

SEPTEMBER (ExB9)

You need: game board, card of 2 different colours, scissors.

First you need to make some playing pieces. Each player needs seven straight pieces (just long enough to connect two points next to each other on the board) and three 'L' pieces, in their own colour:

7 of [   ]   3 of [L-shaped piece]

Take turns to put a piece on the board, one colour joining the circles and the other colour the triangles. The aim is to make a path of your colour across the board with no breaks in it. One colour tries to go from top to bottom, the other from side to side.

If you have put all the pieces on the board and still no-one has made a line, you can pick up one of your pieces at a time and place it anywhere which is empty.

You can make a harder game by drawing a bigger board, making more pieces, and using pieces of different shapes.

TRI BOX (Sp1)

You need: 2 different coloured pencils, scrap paper.

Draw dots as shown below. Take it in turns to join two dots next to each other. If you complete a triangle, put a dot of your colour inside it. The winner is the player with most triangles at the end.

Now try SQUARE BOX – draw the dots in a big square, 5 dots each side, and try to complete each small square.

Now try HEX BOX – draw the dots to make many hexagons, and try to complete each small hexagon.

Then try these with more dots. You might even be able to do it with other shapes (pentagon for a start?)

MATCH PUZZLE (Sp2)

You need: 24 matchsticks.

Set out the matches to make squares like this.

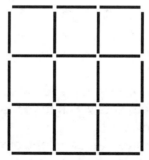

The challenges are:

- take away eight matches and leave two squares
- take away six matches and leave three squares
- take away four matches and leave five squares
- take away eight matches and leave five squares
- take away eight matches and leave three squares
- rearrange all the matches to make one large square
- rearrange all the matches to make two squares.

SIM   (Sp3)

You need: paper, 2 different coloured pencils.

Mark six points on paper in the form of a hexagon:

```
        *    *

     *          *

        *    *
```

Take turns to join any two points with a straight line, using your own colour of pencil. The aim is to make the other player complete a triangle all of their own colour. (The triangle must touch three points of the hexagon – any triangles formed within the hexagon do not count.)

You might want to try this with a pentagon, or other more complicated shapes.

HIP   (Sp4)

You need: paper and pencil.

On the paper, make a 6 x 6 grid of dots:

```
.  .  .  .  .  .
.  .  .  .  .  .
.  .  .  .  .  .
.  .  .  .  .  .
.  .  .  .  .  .
.  .  .  .  .  .
```

One player is X and the other is O. Take turns to put an X or O on a point on the grid. The aim is not to put 4 Xs or Os on points which form the corners of any possible square, while trying to make the other player do it.

Remember that the possible squares can be of any size, and need not be level with the bottom or sides of the grid – they could be tilted squares based on diagonals in the grid.

SPROUTS   (Sp5)

You need: paper and pencil.

An agreed number of dots (perhaps three) is put on a piece of paper. At their turn, a player joins two dots (the line can be long and squiggly) *and* puts a new dot somewhere on the line they have drawn.

A line must not cross another line and no dot can have more than three lines going from it. The first player who cannot make a move loses. It sounds simple, but it isn't – try it!

NIM   (Nu1)

You need: 15 counters.

Put the 15 counters in three piles of four, five and six counters. On your go, you can take one or more counters from one of the piles. The player who takes the very last counter wins.

You can also play this game with 16 counters in four piles of one, three, five and seven counters, when it is known as Marienbad.

DIGITAL NOUGHTS AND CROSSES   (Nu2)

You need: scrap paper, pencils of 2 different colours.

Play noughts and crosses but use the digits (numbers) 1 to 9 instead. Like this:

```
  3  |     | 1
_____|_____|_____
     |     |
     |  2  |
_____|_____|_____
     |     |
  7  |     |
     |     |
```

Each number can be used only once in a game. The winner is the first person to *complete* a line of three numbers which add up to 10.

When you are good at this, you might want to agree that only a line of three numbers which have all been put in by the same player (in the same colour pencil) should win.

Then you might want to make up harder games with bigger squares, larger numbers and higher winning totals.

NAVIGRID   (Nu3)

You need: 2 dice, 2 different coloured pencils, graph paper (large).

Take turns to roll both dice together.

From the starting point of the graph in the bottom left hand corner (0.0), move to the point on the grid shown by the two numbers on the dice. You can use the two numbers in any order you want.

On your next go, move on by the number of squares up and across shown on the dice. Mind you don't fall off the grid!

Mark your route with your coloured pencil. The winner is the first player to the top of the grid.

Once you have got the hang of it, try it on some bigger pieces of squared paper. You can agree on a different winning line or point or sector if you want.

NUMBER RIDDLES (Nu4)

You need: scrap paper and a pencil.

Make up some number riddles to try out on your partner. For example:

- If you double me or square me you get the same result. What number am I?
- If you add me to another number it makes no difference. What number am I?
- If I multiply another number, it makes no difference. What number am I?
- I have two digits and the first is bigger than the second. If you add my digits the result is 16. If you subtract my digits the result is 2. What number am I?

You can make these harder and harder as you both get better at it.

ALIEN EIGHT FINGER (OCTAL) ARITHMETIC (Nu5)

You need: scrap paper, pencil.

We count in tens because we have ten fingers. If we lived in another world where everybody had eight fingers, we would count in eights. In this strange arithmetic, there would be no word or symbol for '9', and '10' would mean one '8' and no units (just as it means one '10' and no units in our base-ten or decimal system). In the same way, '12' would mean one '8' and two units, '23' would mean two '8's and three units, and '100' would mean one lot of 8 times 8 (or 8^2) (as it means one lot of 10 times 10 (or 10^2) in our system).

Try translating some examples in this base-8 system to our earth base-10 system: 11, 6, 17, 42, 15, 26, 51, 34 . . . Now try some harder ones.

You will need to help each other to work these out – one to hold up fingers and the other to count!

How would you tell an eight-fingered visitor the answers to these questions using their own base-8 number system:

- How many days in a fortnight?
- How many hours in a day?
- How many days in January?
- How many minutes in an hour?

You can make up many more and harder questions to try on each other, as well as number riddles. Then you might discover a world where the people have only six fingers, and have to start again working out a base-6 system!

SPLITS (Nu6)

You need: 50 counters.

Put an agreed number of counters in an agreed number of piles. You might want to start with less than 50 counters, and perhaps only one pile. Players take turns to divide any pile into two *unequal* piles (so piles of one or two counters can't be played). The winner is the last player who can make an allowed move.

Now try the game dividing only into *equal* piles. Then try it with a choice at each turn of dividing into equal piles *or* combining two unequal piles to make a larger pile.

PIG (Nu7)

You need: 2 dice, paper and pencil.

In a turn you can throw the two dice as often as you want, keeping a note of the total of the numbers thrown. You can choose to stop at any time and bank the total so far. However, if you throw a 1, *all* your score for that turn is lost, and the turn ends. The first player to reach 200 points wins.

THE 57 GAME (Nu8)

You need: paper, pencil, a counter or coin.

Draw a big magic square just like this one:

6	7	2
1	5	9
8	3	4

A magic square is a number square in which all the rows and columns and diagonals add up to the same total, using all the numbers starting from one.

The first player puts the counter on any square and counts the number as a starting total. The second player moves the coin to another square which is *not in the same row or column* as the first position, and adds that number to the total.

If you bring the total to exactly 57, you win the game. If you are forced to go further than 57, you lose the game.

DOUBLE OR TAKE (Nu9)

You need: paper and pencil.

Player A chooses any number (e.g. 76). Player B can either double it or take away a square number (i.e. a number which is the result of multiplying a smaller number by itself) or cube number (i.e. a number which is the result of multiplying a smaller number by itself then by itself again). Player A then takes their turn in the same way. The aim is to be the player to reach zero.

BIRTHDAYS (Pu1)

You need: scrap paper, pencil.

You can work out the day of the week on which you were born like this:

1. Take the last two figures of the year in which you were born.
2. Divide by 12, note the result and write down the number left over (remainder).
3. Divide the number left over by four and note the result.
4. Write down the number of the day of the month you were born on.
5. Add up the result of the divisions in steps 2 and 3, the remainder from step 2 and your birth day number from step 4.
6. Add the right number for your birthday month:

January 1	April 2	July 0	October 1
February 4	May 2	August 3	November 4
March 4	June 5	September 6	December 6

   If you were born in January or February of a leap year, subtract one.
7. Divide by seven. What is left over?
8. Look at the left-over number from step 7 and match it to a day:

Saturday 0	Monday 2	Wednesday 4	Friday 6
Sunday 1	Tuesday 3	Thursday 5	

   That is the day you were born on!
9. Ask your friends for their dates of birth and work out what day they were born on. Which was the most popular day to be born?

VANISHING SQUARES (Pu2)

You need: scrap paper, pencil.

This square is called a vanishing square:

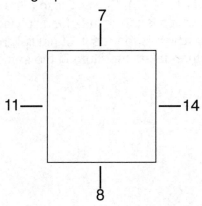

Copy it on to a piece of paper and join the numbers by drawing another square inside the first one. Find the difference between each pair of joined numbers and write it on the sides of the new square. Go on doing this, and in the end you will get a square in the middle with zero on each side.

Now try making some vanishing number squares of your own. It is not as hard as it looks!

RELATIONS   (Pu3)

You need: scrap paper, pencil.

Patrick has lots of relations. His grandmother on his father's side had two children, who each had two children. His grandmother on his mother's side had three children, one of whom had no children, one of whom had two children and one of whom had four children.

How many cousins does Patrick have?

You will probably need to draw a family tree or diagram to map out these relations.

When you have drawn a family tree for Patrick, you will be able to think up other relations puzzles to try on your friends. Then try making puzzles based on the invented family tree of a new person. You could also try drawing your own family tree.

RABBIT RELATIONS   (Pu4)

You need: scrap paper, pencil – and some rabbits might help!

You are given a pair of baby rabbits. After two months they produce another pair of rabbits and they go on producing a new pair every month after that. Each new pair of rabbits produces a further new pair after two months and goes on producing a new pair every month after that.

You will need to draw a family tree for the rabbits to map out their relations. If you were given the rabbits as a New Year's Day present, how many rabbits will you have by the beginning of July? September? December?

This comes from a book published in 1202 by an Italian mathematician called Fibonacci (say the 'cc' as 'ch'). The number of pairs of rabbits alive each month make a sequence known as the Fibonacci sequence, which seems to crop up all over the place when you know of it. Each new number in the sequence is found by adding the two previous numbers. Write out the numbers in the Fibonacci sequence. How many rabbits would you have by New Year's Day two years later?!

DETECTIVE   (Pu5)

You need: scrap paper, pencil.

Mr and Mrs Robinson have two children. Michael is 18 and goes to work; Susan is 12 and goes to school. One day their house was burgled while no-one was at home.

They all had to give statements to the police:

- Dad said: I left home at 0815 to go to work and came back home at 1650. I came home for dinner at 1330 and was home for 55 minutes.
- Mum said: I went to the shops from 1020 until 1115, and went to see a friend from 1300 until 1420.
- Michael said: I left home for work at 1105 and didn't get back until 1900.
- Susan said: I left for school at 0830, but I felt sick and came home at 1245. I was there all afternoon except for 25 minutes when I went to my friend's house to ask about homework. I left the house at 1350.

When was the burglar in the house gathering his swag?

ADDITION PUZZLE (Pu6)

You need: scrap paper, pencil.

Try to use all of the numbers from 1 to 7, using each only once, to make an addition sum with a total of 100.

PENNY SOLITAIRE (Pu7)

You need to make a game board on a piece of paper, but it is only six rows of six points, connected by lines up, across and diagonal. You also need six counters or small coins.

The counters must be placed on points so that no two counters are connected by a straight line.

This game was sold in London for one (old) penny at the end of the last century – and can be played with pennies.

UNITED SHIRTS (Pu8)

You need: scrap paper, pencil.

Your local football club has just enough players for two teams, with six reserves for each team. Their shirts are numbered (on one side only) from 1 to 34.

How many figure 1s are needed for their new set of shirts? Can you think of any more football shirt problems to try on your friends?

What other numbers will be needed? What if there were more players or teams? What if there were shirts to be made for a rugby union or rugby league or hockey or lacrosse team?

MAGIC SQUARES

You need: paper and pencil.

A magic square is a number square in which all the rows and columns and diagonals add up to the same total. All the numbers starting from one must be used. The first magic square is thought to have been found in China in 2800 BC.

There is only one magic square with three numbers per row or column:

6	7	2
1	5	9
8	3	4

If you think you have found another, you will find it is actually a rotation or reflection of this one.

There are about 880 different 4 x 4 magic squares – how many can you find? You could start by completing this one. All rows, columns and diagonals add up to 34.

	3		14
8			12
11		6	

There are thought to be about 13 million 5 x 5 magic squares. Even larger ones are possible.

BLOCKSAW

You need: scrap paper, pencil.

A wooden cubic building brick is painted a different colour on every surface. Each of its sides is 50 cm long. The cube is sawn into smaller cubes with sides 10 cm long.

How many smaller cubes are there? How many of the smaller cubes have at least one painted surface? How many have one painted surface? How many have two, how many three, etc?

It will help if you draw the big cube. Can you make up other problems like this to try on your friends?

THE TOWER OF BRAHMA (Ex1)

You need to make 8 circles of card in 8 different sizes, cut out and each circle coloured a different colour. You might want to make three flat card storage bases or 'pegs' as well.

The original Tower of Brahma puzzle was made of three pegs standing in a base board and eight discs of different sizes, each with a hole in the middle.

You start with all eight discs in a pile in order of size, biggest at the bottom and smallest on the top.

Only one disc can be moved at a time. It must be the disc on top of a pile. It must be placed on one of the other storage places ('peg') before another is moved. Also, a larger disc can never be placed on a smaller disc.

You have to move all the discs from the start position on the middle peg to one of the other pegs to finish with the same arrangement in order of size, using only the other two storage pegs.

If starting with eight seems too hard, try with fewer.

See if you can predict the least number of moves to finish. How many moves to finish a tower of 10 discs or 20 discs?

The story is that the priests of the temple of Brahma in Benares in Northern India had 64 golden discs and three diamond pegs. How many moves would they have taken?!

INSTRUCTIONS FOR CARD GAMES

SWEET SIXTEEN (CG1)

You need: pack of cards, scrap paper, pencil.

Ace = 1, Jack = 11, Queen = 12, King = 13. Deal seven cards each. Put the rest of the pack face-down.

Aim to take 'tricks' by being the one to play the card that brings the total value of the cards already played in that turn to 16.

If you win a trick, you lead the next trick. If you can't play a card without going over 16, you must draw card(s) from the stock pile (unseen) until you can.

The winner is the first person to get rid of all their cards.

You might want to play several games, keeping a record of how many tricks each of you won in each game, then add them up to decide the overall winner.

POKER

You need: pack of cards.

Each player is dealt five cards face down.

On your turn you can decide to trade in one, two or three of your cards for new ones. When everyone has had one turn, you show your cards. Or you may decide to have two turns before showing. The aim of the game is to put together in your hand sets of cards of high value.

The order of value, from the lowest to the highest, is:

- pair
- two pairs
- three of a kind
- full house (a pair and three of a kind)
- four of a kind
- low flush (sequence 9, 10, Jack, Queen, King)
- Royal Flush (sequence 10, Jack, Queen, King, Ace)
- five of a kind.

You may decide that deuces (2s) are wild, and can stand for any other card. This is the traditional cowboy game! They bet on whether their hand will win on any one round, before showing their cards.

Another good card game is Casino, but the instructions are much more complicated. If you like these card games, you might want to find out the rules for Casino from the library.

TOUGH BEANS

You need: pack of cards.

Ace = 1, Jack = 11, Queen = 12, King = 13. Deal eight cards each. Put the rest of the pack face-down, then turn the top card face-up separately.

The first player plays any card next to the face-up card, so that the value of both can be seen.

The second player must put down any number of cards whose total value is equal to the sum or the difference of the two face-up cards. You must show the cards you intend to play, then put them together and put them face-up on one of the cards that was already face-up on the table – so there are still only two face-up cards showing. Then the first player goes again.

If you cannot go when it is your turn, you must pick up cards from the face-down pile until you can. The winner is the first player to get rid of all their cards.

WHAT'S MY RULE? (CG4)

You need: pack of cards.

Agree that Ace, Jack, Queen, King can count 1, 11, 12, 13 as well as being picture cards. The first player arranges the pack of cards (or just a part of it if you wish) in a sequence or order following a rule or rules which he or she has thought up. Examples could be: if the last card is even the next is odd, if the last card is from 1 to 7 the next is from 8 to 13, and so on.

The deck is then placed face-down and the other player turns over the top card and tries to predict what the next card will be. Keep turning cards over until you can always predict the next card correctly.

The number of wrong predictions becomes the first player's score. Now change round so the second player arranges the pack, and so on. As you get better at this you will use more complicated rules.

This is a simpler version of a game called Eleusis, which goes faster with three or four rather than two players. In this, the dealer makes up the secret rule, then deals out all the cards equally to the other players. Players take turns to put a card face-up in the middle. The dealer says whether the card played obeys the rule or not. If it obeys the rule, it is left there to help everyone work out what the rule is. If it does not, the player must take it back. The winner is the first to say what the rule is – and be right!

MULTIPLES RUMMY (CG5)

You need: pack of cards.

Ace = 1, Jack = 11, Queen = 12, King = 13. Shuffle the pack and deal five cards to each player. Put the rest of the pack face-down on the table. Turn over the top card and put it down separately to start a (face-up) discard pile.

The object of the game is to get rid of your cards by putting down sets of three which add up to multiples of the same number, such as 3, 15, 21 or 5, 10, 20.

If you can't go, you must pick up the top card from either the face-up pile or (without looking) the face-down pile. If you now have a set of three, put it down. Whether you have a set or not, put any one of your cards down on the face-up pile.

The winner is the one who gets rid of all their cards first. You can also score by having the other player(s) add up the numbers on the cards they have left, so after several games the overall winner is the player with the lowest total score.

MATHS PONTOON (CG6)

You need: pack of 40 cards without the Jacks, Queens, Kings; 20 counters; a made-up set of five 'operations' cards showing + − x ÷ =.

This game is more fun with three or four players. Each player has three counters to start and the rest are left in a central 'bank'. One player is the dealer and holds the bank. The playing cards are shuffled and four dealt to each player (the rest are put face-down in the centre of the table).

On their turn, each player must use all their four cards together with an equals card and any other operations cards to make a 'sum' which is correct. If the other players agree it is correct, the player can take one more counter from the central bank.

If a player cannot make a sum with the cards in their hand, they must pay one counter out of their own supply to the central bank. The winner is the first player to reach a total of 10 counters. If the game goes on, this player will become the new dealer and banker.

66

ELEVENSES (CS1)

You need: a pack of 40 cards without the Jacks, Queens and Kings.

The player deals out eight cards face-up, and looks for pairs of cards which add up to 11. When you find such a pair you deal a new card onto both, and go on like this until all the cards are used up – or you get stuck!

FIFTY-FIVE (CS2)

You need: a pack of 40 cards without the Jacks, Queens and Kings.

The player lays out ten piles of four cards face-up – but at any one time you can only see the top card of each pile.

The aim is to get the top cards showing a total of 55. To do this you can move the top card of any pile onto the top of any other pile.

SEVENS (CS3)

You need: a pack of 40 cards without the Jacks, Queens and Kings.

The cards are dealt out face-up in a row, looking for 7s and any consecutive (next to each other) runs of cards which add up to 7 (e.g. 4 and 3) or a multiple of 7 (14, 21, 28, etc).

Single 7s and runs of additions or multiples are taken out. The aim is to take out all the cards in this way.

THE THIRTY-SIX SQUARE (CS4)

You need: a pack of 36 cards without the Jacks, Queens, Kings and Aces.

The puzzle is to arrange the 36 cards in a 6 x 6 square so that:

- the total of each row is 36,
- the total of each column is 36,
- no two cards of the same number are in the same row, column or diagonal,
- each row and each column has three red and three black cards,
- one diagonal is made up of only red cards, and one of only black cards.

CALCULATION (CS5)

You need: pack of cards.

This is also known as Broken Intervals. Choose any Ace, 2, 3, and 4 and lay them in a row facing up as 'foundation cards'. All the rest of the cards, kept face-down, are called the stock. As the game goes on, four piles for throwing down cards (discard piles) will be made next to the foundation cards.

The aim is to build on each foundation card in this order:

1. On Ace, every card: Ace, 2, 3, 4, 5, 6, 7, 8, 9, 10, J, Q, K.
2. On 2, every second card: 2, 4, 6, 8, 10, Q, Ace, 3, 5, 7, 9, J, K.
3. On 3, every third card: 3, 6, 9, Q, 2, 5, 8, J, Ace, 4, 7, 10, K.
4. On 4, every fourth card: 4, 8, Q, 3, 7, J, 2, 6, 10, Ace, 5, 9, K.

To play, one card at a time is turned face-up from the top of the stock pile, and is put overlapping any of the foundation cards if it fits there in the sequence, to start building. If a card cannot be used to build, it may be put face-up on any of the four discard piles. As the game goes on, the top card of any discard pile may also be used to build, but may not be transferred to another discard pile.

The skill lies in controlling the cards in the discard piles. For example, Kings will be needed to build last of all, so it will be helpful to keep them either all in one pile or at the bottom of each pile. Try to build cards on the discard piles in the backwards order they will be needed to build on the foundation cards. Also, you might want to try to get cards of the same rank spread out through the different discard piles. If a discard pile runs out, the space can be filled with a new pile, but you can't have more than four discard piles.

GO (StB1)

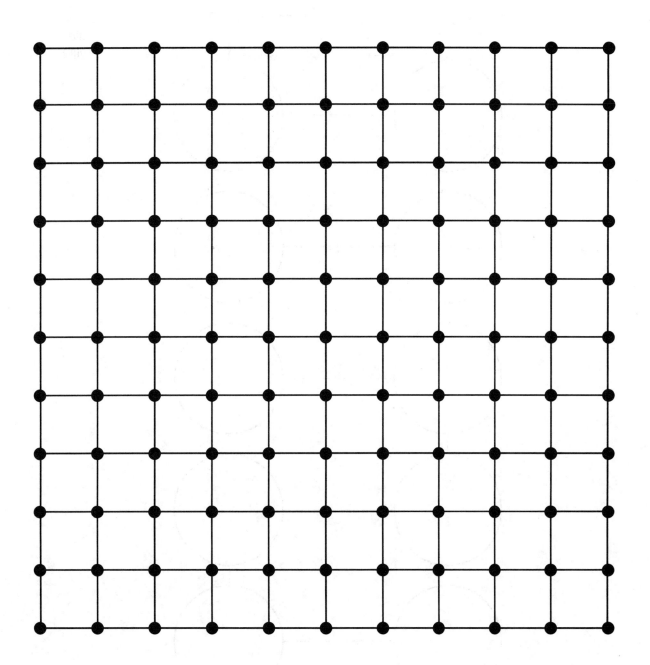

MATCHING MIN (StB2)

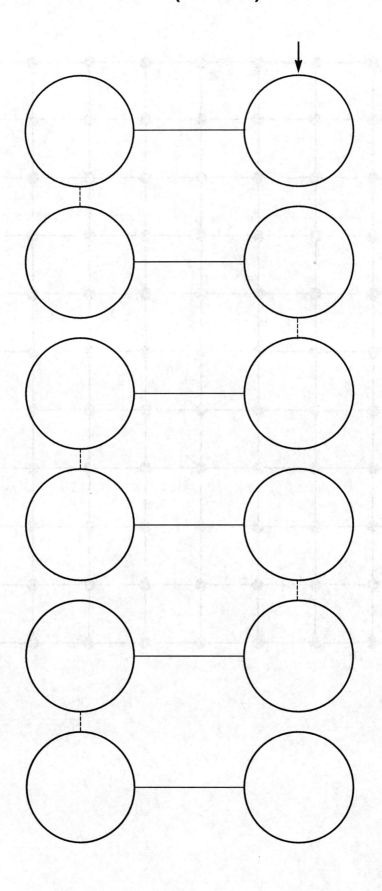

PALM TREE (StB3)

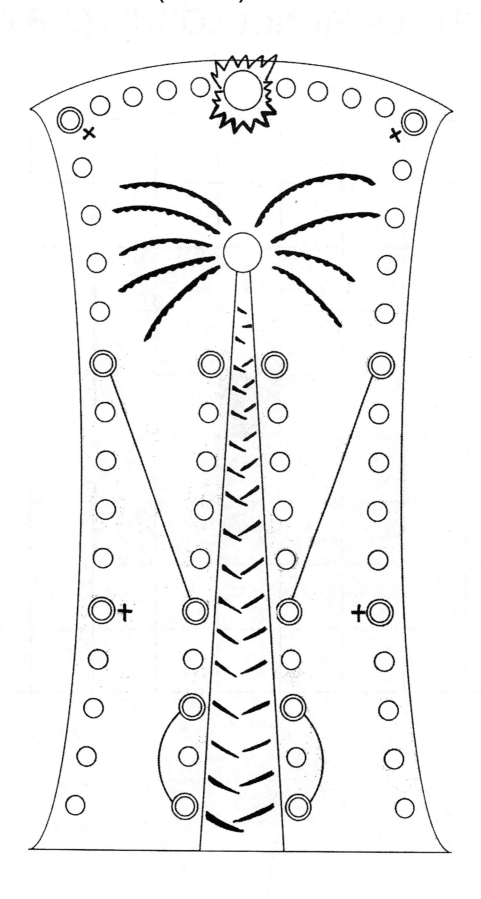

SEEGA (StB4)
LUDUS LATRUNCULORUM (StB5)

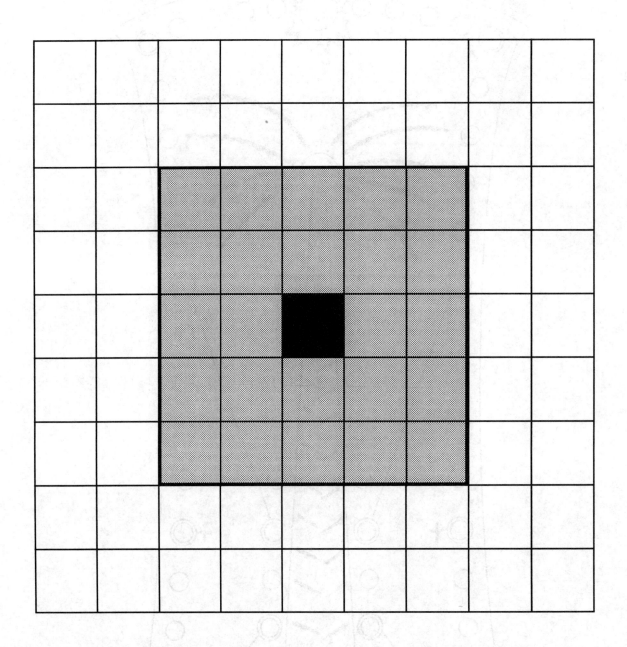

PATOLLI (StB6)

KONO (StB7)

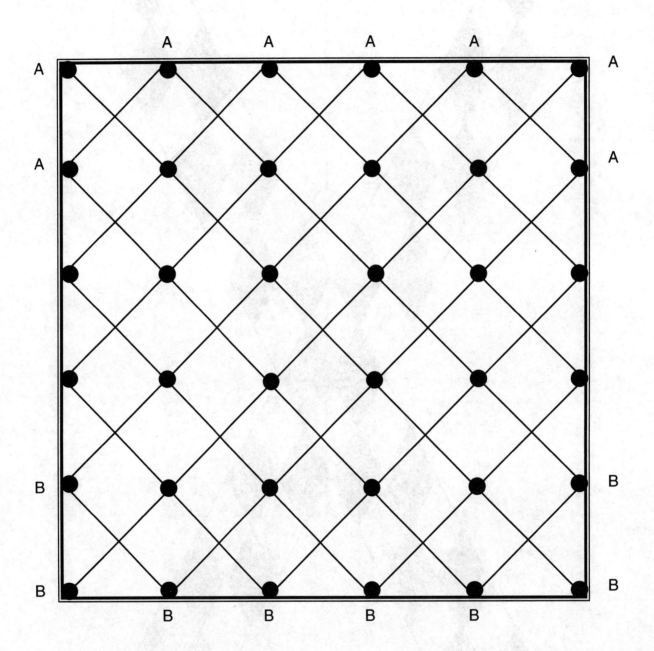

KUNGSER (StB8)

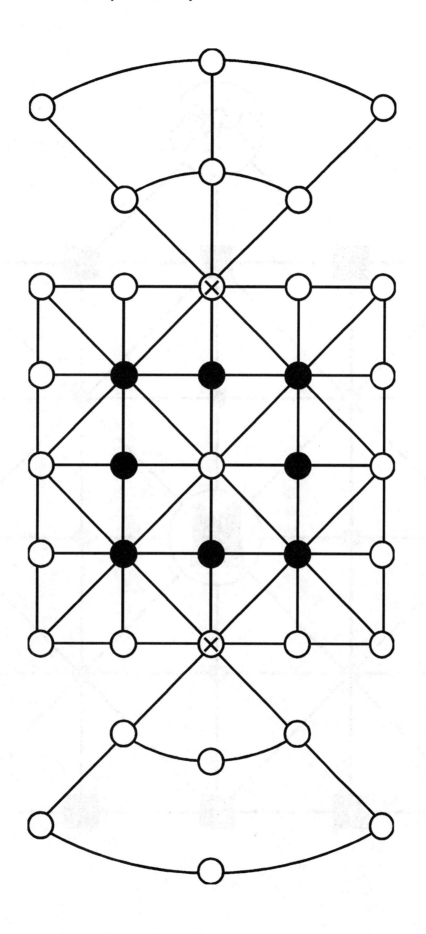

THE REBEL (StB9)

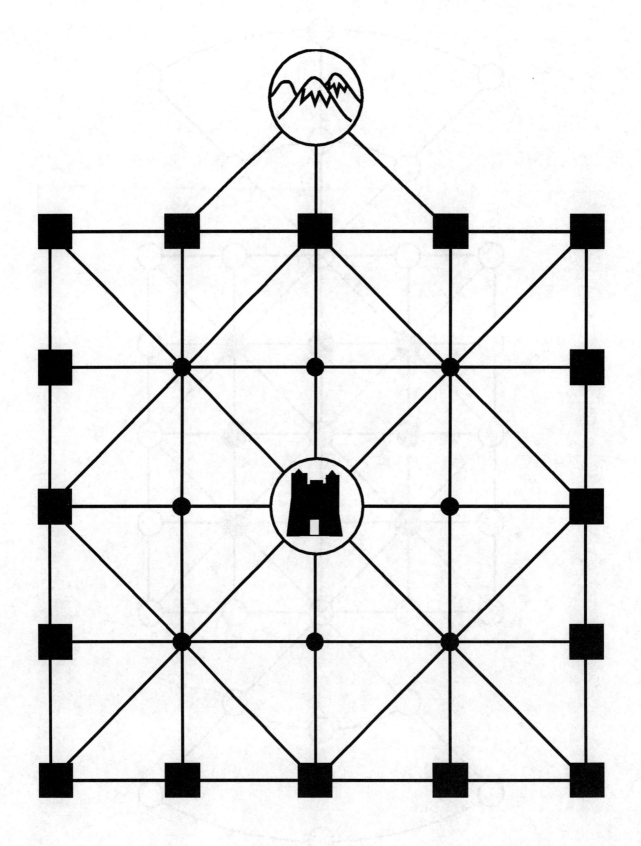

CHINESE CHECKERS (StB10)

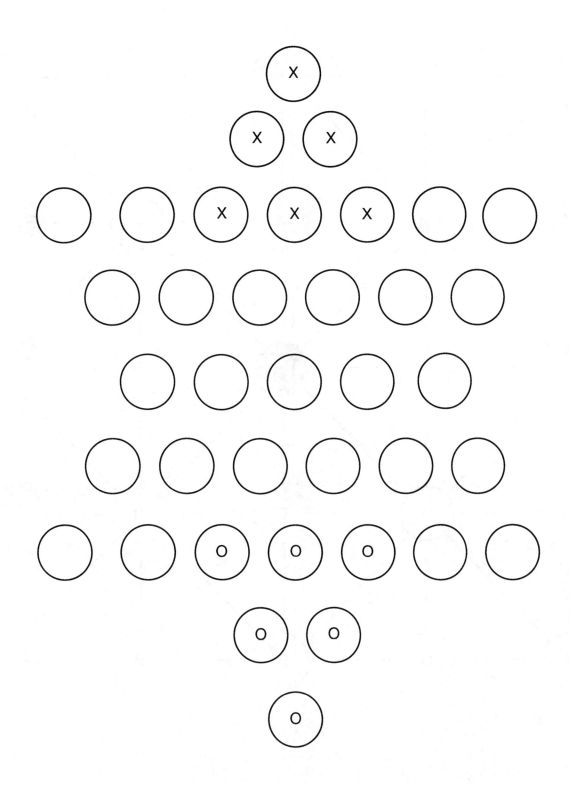

ALQUERQUE (SpB1)

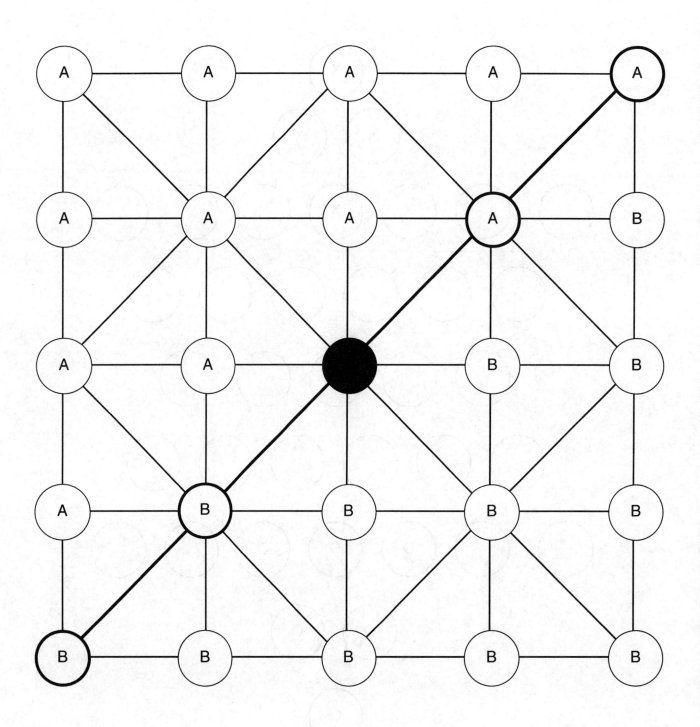

FOX AND GEESE (SpB2)
SOLITAIRE (PuB1)

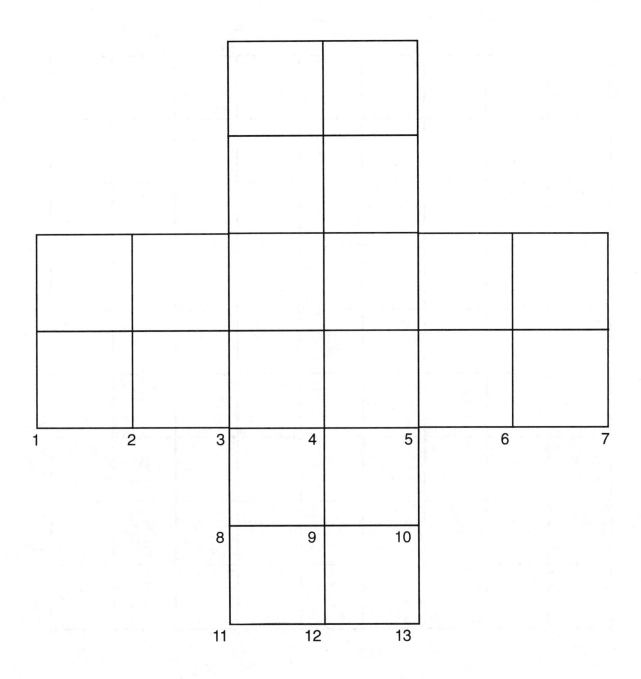

HASAMI SHOGI (SpB3)

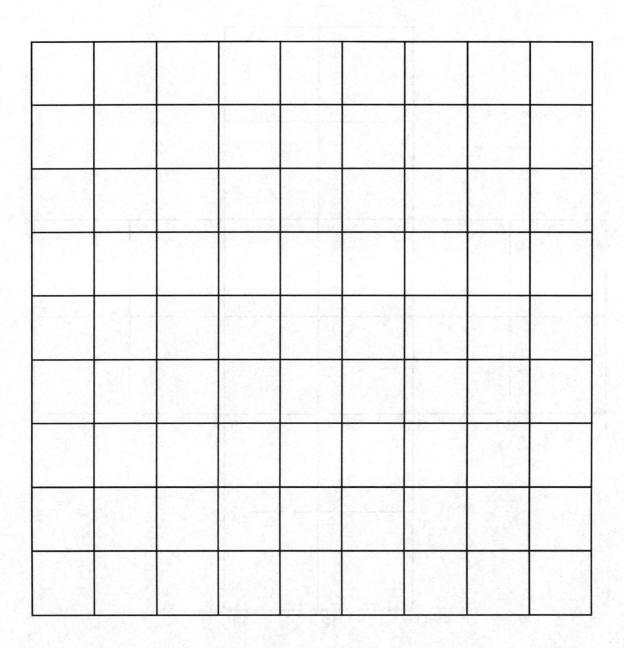

MAZES (SpB4)

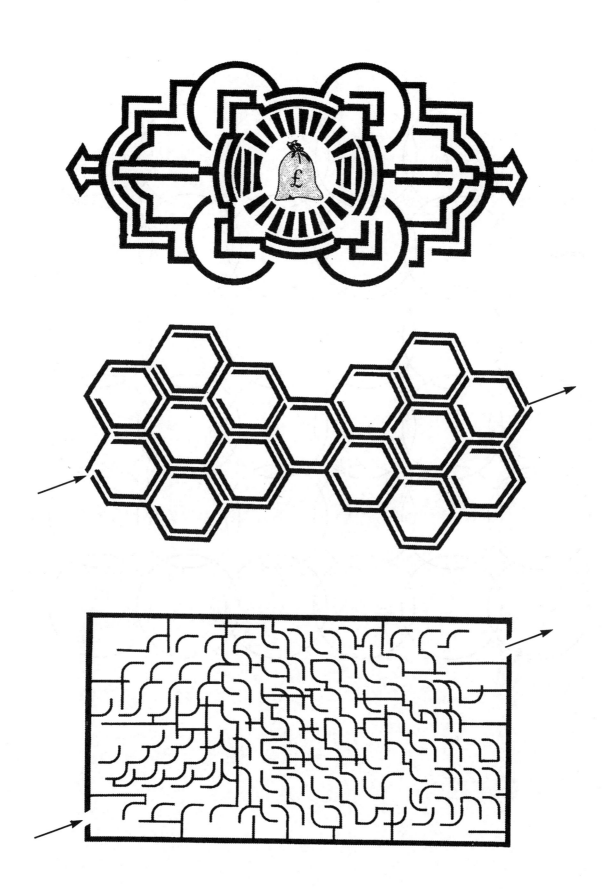

PATHWAY (SpB5)

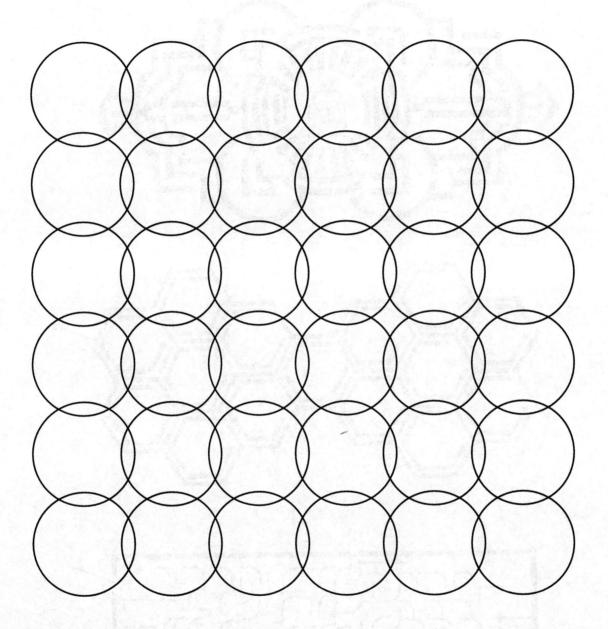

AVOID (SpB6)

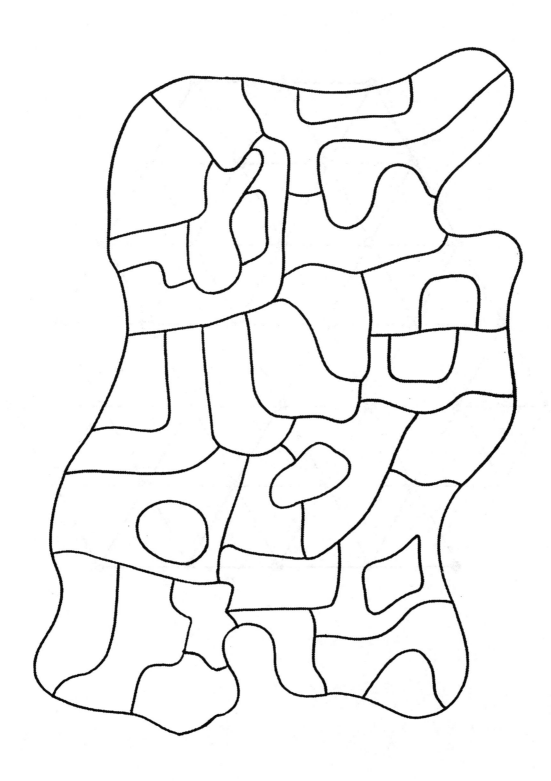

TRIADS (SpB7)

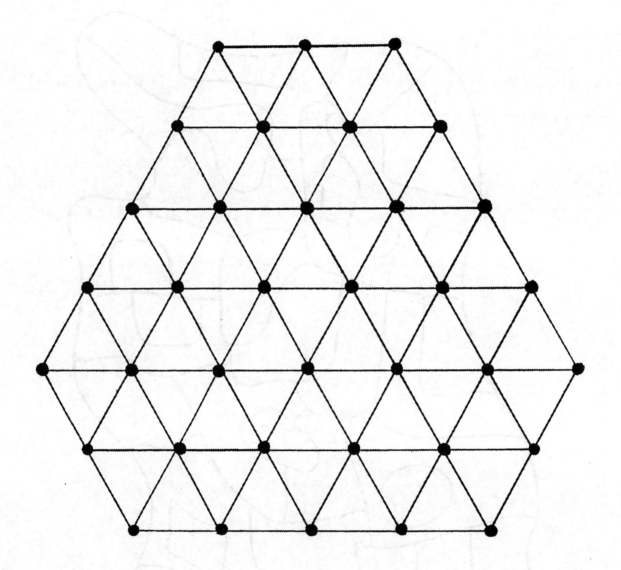

SZ'KWA (SpB8)

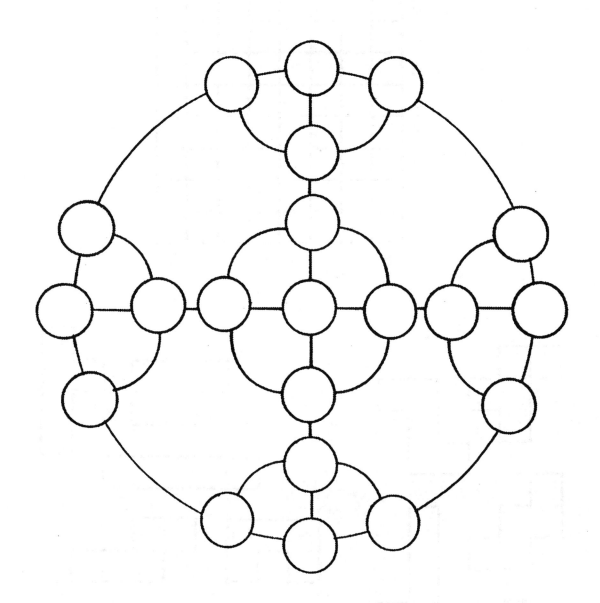

PENTOMINOS (SpB9)

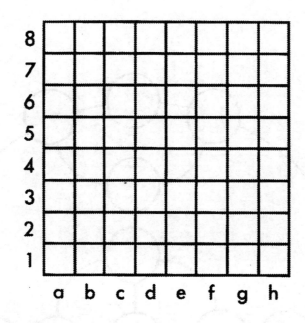

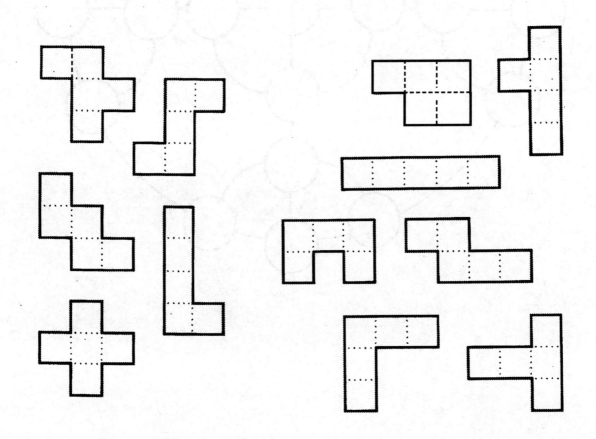

QUADS (SpB10)

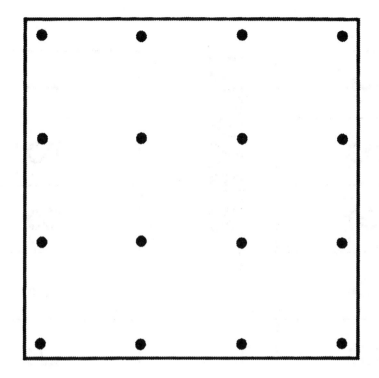

Blue				
Yellow				
Red				
Green				

COMBINATIONS (NuB1)

PLAYER 1

1	2	3	4	5	6	7	8	9	10	11	12

PLAYER 2

1	2	3	4	5	6	7	8	9	10	11	12

SIDEWINDER (NuB2)

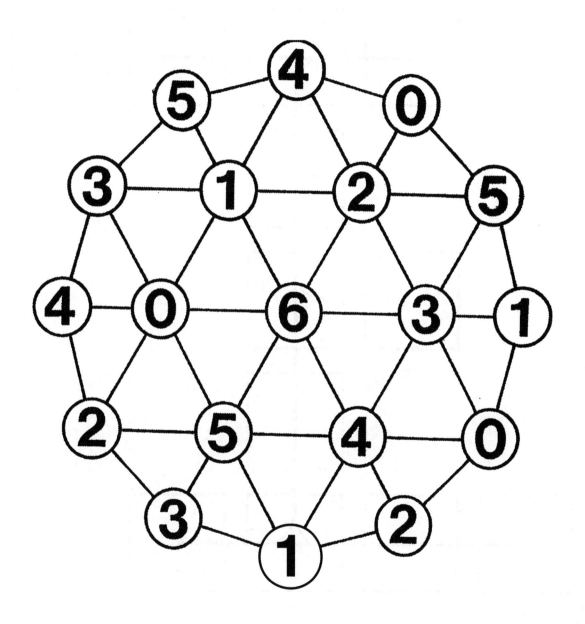

SHUNT (PuB2)

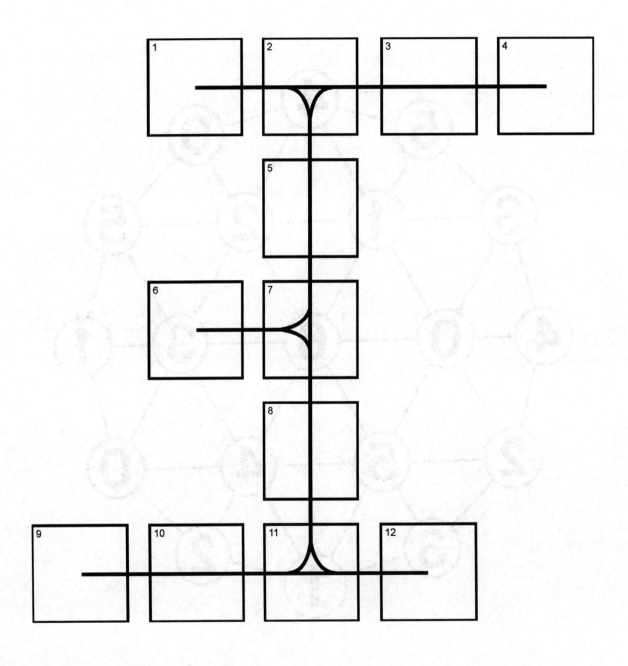

ALL CHANGE (PuB3)

	1	
2	3	4
5	6	7
	8	

PENTALPHA (PuB4)

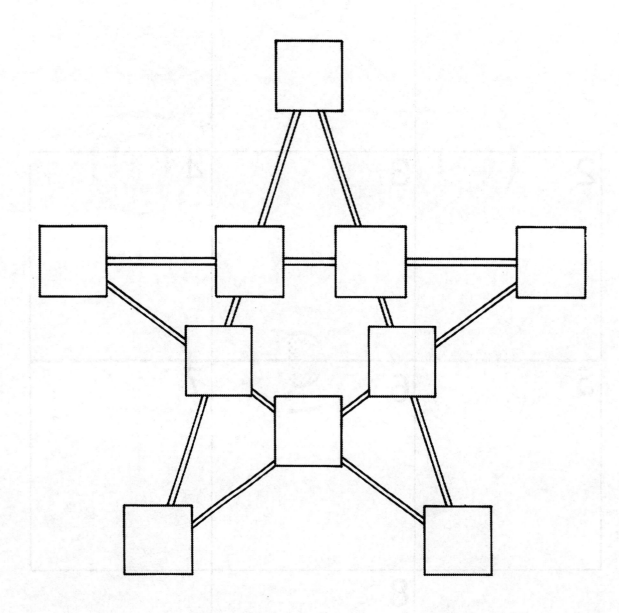

TREBLE INTERCHANGE (PuB5)

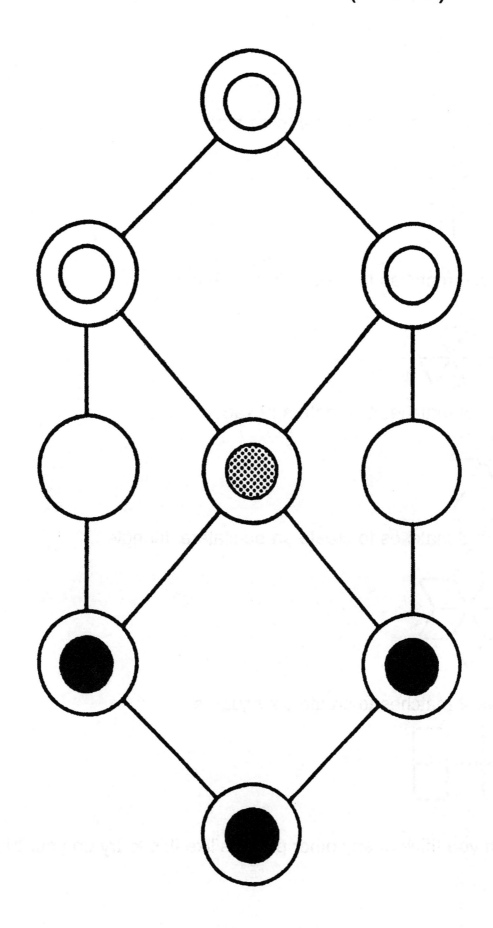

STICK AT IT (PuB6)

Move 3 matches to create three squares

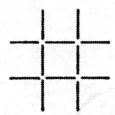

Move 6 matches to create six rhombuses

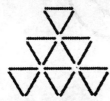

Move 4 matches to create a hexagon

Move 6 matches to create an equilateral triangle

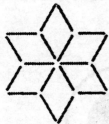

Move 2 matches to create six squares

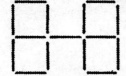

Can you think of any other puzzles like this to try on your friends?

MARVELLOUS 26 (PuB7)

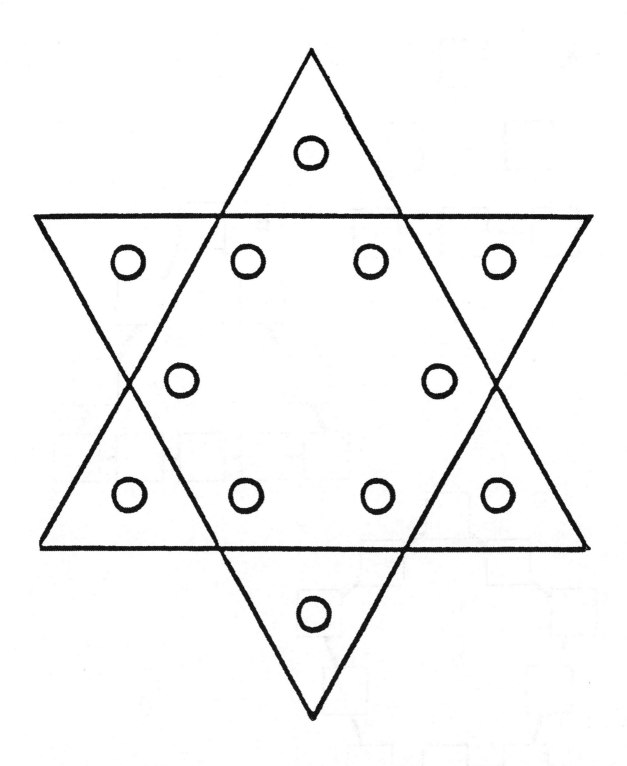

MAGIC TRIANGLES (PuB8)

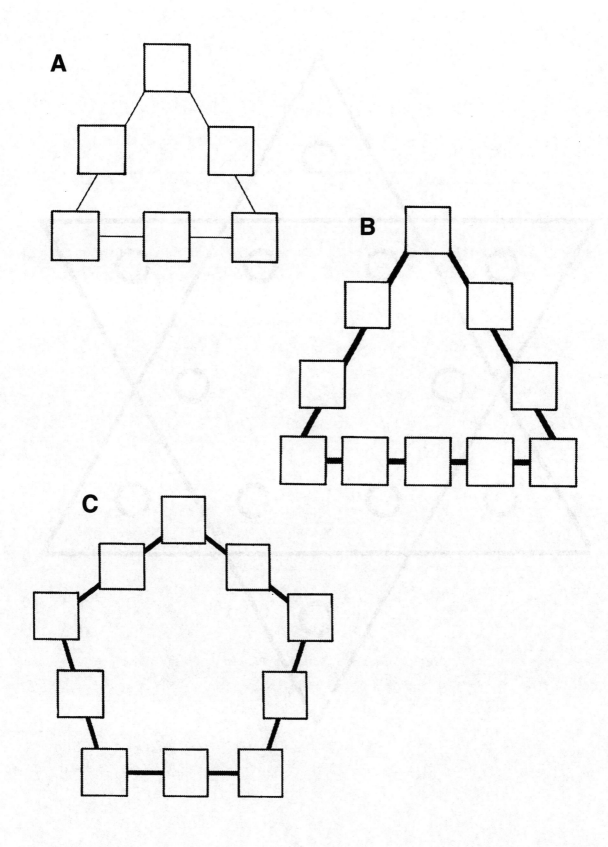

OLD FARMER PUZZLE (PuB9)

MANCALA – WARI (ExB1)
MANCALA – GONGCLAK (ExB2)

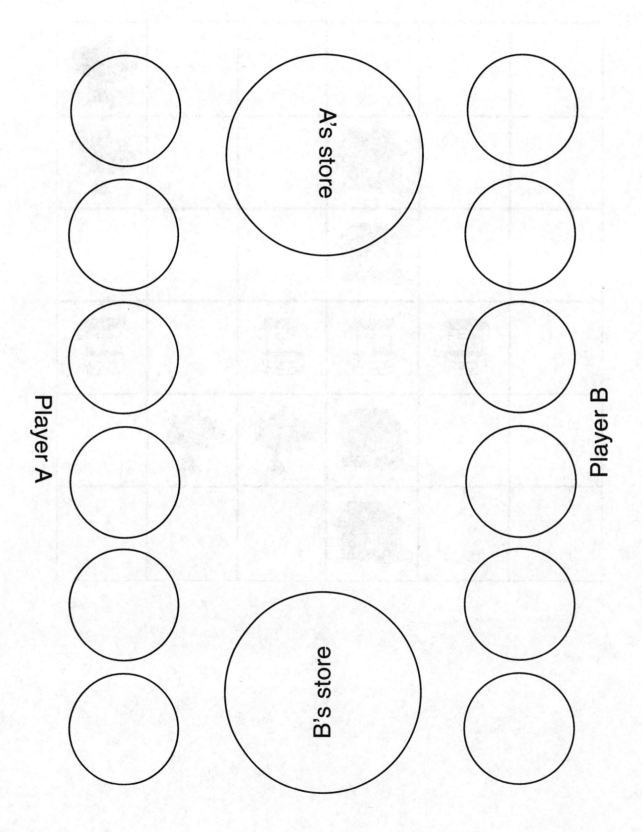

TABULA (ExB3)

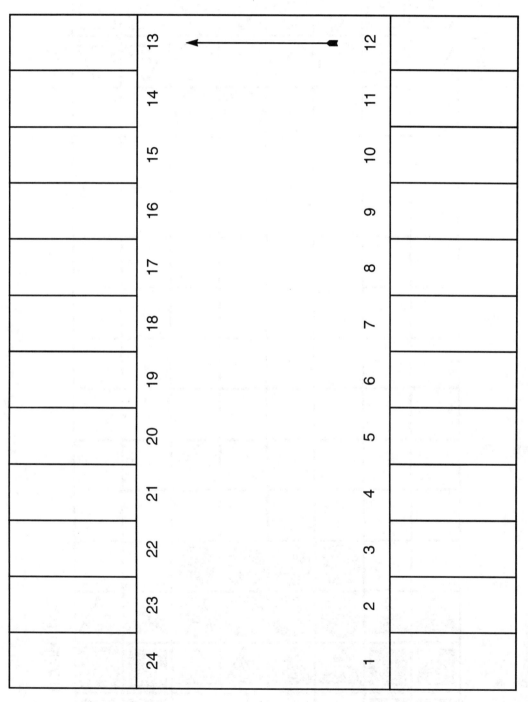

RITHMOMACHIA (ExB4)

Even (White)

Odd (Black)

289 169 81 25
153 91 72 42 20 6 45 15
81 49 64 36 16 4 25 9
8 6 4 2

3 5 7 9
16 36 9 25 49 81 64 100
28 66 12 30 56 90 120 190
49 121 225 361

LATINO (ExB5)
LAP (ExB7)

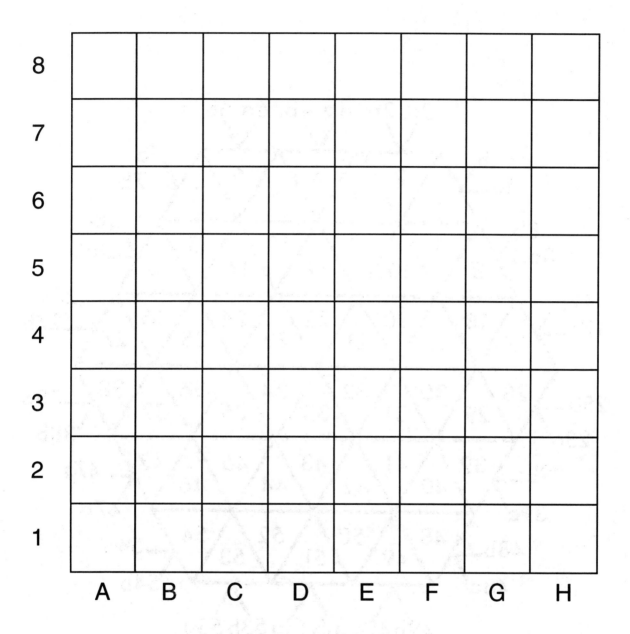

RAYBOX (ExB6)

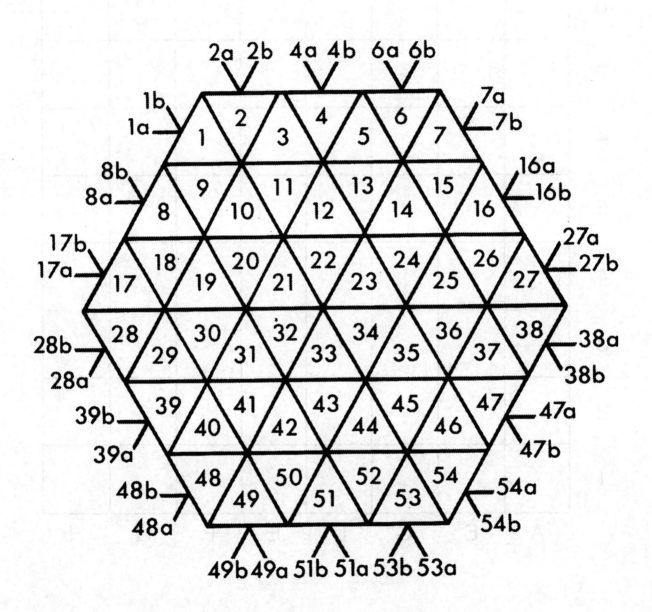

ENTROPY (ExB8)

SEPTEMBER (ExB9)